THIS I
BELIEVE

THIS I
BELIEVE

On Love

EDITED BY DAN GEDIMAN
WITH JOHN GREGORY
AND MARY JO GEDIMAN

WILEY

John Wiley & Sons, Inc.

Copyright © 2011 by This I Believe, Inc. All rights reserved

This I Believe ® is a registered trademark of This I Believe, Inc.

Published by John Wiley & Sons, Inc., Hoboken, New Jersey
Published simultaneously in Canada

Design by Forty-five Degree Design LLC

For general information about our other products and services, please contact our Customer Care Department within the United States at (800) 762-2974, outside the United States at (317) 572-3993 or fax (317) 572-4002.

Wiley also publishes its books in a variety of electronic formats. Some content that appears in print may not be available in electronic books. For more information about Wiley products, visit our web site at www.wiley.com.

Library of Congress Cataloging-in-Publication Data:
This I believe : on love / [edited by] Dan Gediman with John Gregory and Mary Jo Gediman.
   p. cm.
   ISBN 978-0-470-87268-0 (cloth : alk.paper); ISBN 978-0-470-90076-5 (ebk);
ISBN 978-0-470-90077-2 (ebk); ISBN 978-0-470-90078-9 (ebk)
   I. Love. I. Gediman, Dan. II. Gregory, John. III. Gediman, Mary Jo.
BF575.L8T53 2010
177'.7—dc22

2010028347

To Margot Trevor Wheelock,
who was responsible for
This I Believe

CONTENTS

Introduction

The idea for *This I Believe* began in the early 1950s when Edward R. Murrow and three fellow businessmen decided that during that particular time of economic uncertainty and the shadow of war, there was a strong need for Americans to take an inventory of their personal beliefs and find the seeds of their strength and happiness. A radio series was born that would feature a chosen number of men and women who would unfold their philosophies of life and share what they deemed important.

During that period, from 1951 to 1955, people wrote of the importance of freedom, hope for the future, and the necessity of personal virtues, such as goodness, kindness, and integrity. They also wrote of love—love of country, love of God, and love of family and friends.

Almost exactly fifty years later, in 2004, we created a nonprofit organization to reawaken this project and re-create *This I Believe*. We, too, asked men and women to write of their personal beliefs. We, too, created a radio series to share those beliefs with others.

When we first went on the air in April 2005 and asked listeners to send in their own *This I Believe* essays, we were overwhelmed by the response. To date, we have received more than ninety thousand essays—from every U.S. state and more than ninety countries; from conservatives and liberals; from women and men; from all nationalities and creeds; from every stage of life—kindergartner to senior citizen.

During this period of the early twenty-first century, we, too, have found that there are common themes among the essays submitted to *This I Believe*. People today still write of the importance of goodness, kindness, and a hope for the future. They still write of the importance of freedom and integrity. And they still write of the importance of love— which brings us to the book that you now hold in your hands.

In this collection, you will find essays that touch on many different aspects of love, including some you might not quickly associate with the word. We suspect that when many of us hear the word *love*, what first comes to mind is romantic love, and we certainly have some wonderful essays in this volume on that subject. But the subject of love encompasses so much more.

There is the love that one feels for one's parents and siblings, the love for one's children, friends, and neighbors. There is the love people have for their pets, their teachers, their homes. There is love of nature, of place. There are essays on the power of love. From a doctor, we have an essay about the power of love to heal a hurting body. And a young woman writes about the power of love to help her overcome drug addiction.

In these essays, people have also explored the darker side of love. Of how hard it is to love your enemies, estranged parents, ex-spouses, difficult family members. How love isn't always what one thought or hoped it would be.

Some write about the unique ways they show their love for others or that others have shown for them—through knitting socks, baking bread, hunting ducks.

Clearly, love is one of the most powerful and universal of human emotions.

In reading and rereading these essays in preparation for this book, we've been struck by how such widely diverse views on love can touch us in varying ways from day to day. That's the beauty of love—it resonates differently in each of us, and each of these sixty essayists, whether they are students or retirees, single mothers or longtime fathers, offer us their own unique ways of loving and being loved. In their intimate and honest stories, these essayists share acts of hope and faith, reflections on grief and loss, and celebrations of acceptance and forgiveness.

We hope you enjoy this collection and take the opportunity to share it with someone you love. It is an affirmation of the strong and everlasting bonds between us.

The Love I Choose

∽

JESSICA MERCER ZERR

My husband gets up first to shower, giving me an extra twenty minutes to sleep. He wakes me with a kiss on my forehead and whispers he loves me. Then he leaves without turning on any lights, so I get five more minutes. He unloads the dishwasher and makes the decaf coffee we began drinking when we decided to start trying to conceive more than a year ago. When I emerge from my shower, my coffee is ready—two sugars, cream—and he hands me the paper. We speak little. *Morning Edition* and old-fashioned oatmeal bubble in the background.

At the end of the day, I cook supper, giving my husband half an hour to watch the news without interruption. After the weather report, he sits down at the table and watches while I finish cooking our meal. We eat and talk. Mostly we talk about what has to be done—groceries to buy, grass to mow, bills to pay—and I mention that the door still sticks. After dinner, if the weather is nice, we go for a walk, maybe watch a little TV. Bedtime comes at nine-thirty. When the lights are out, we confess the things that worry us, drawing strength from each other's nearness.

I believe this is love.

When I was a child I thought a lot about what it means to love. I knew the romantic ideals of Cinderella and Sleeping Beauty, but it was the love story of Laura Ingalls and Almanzo Wilder that I returned to again and again. In contrast, their love story was so stark and so deliberate, and it alone continued beyond the ever after.

I once asked my mother if she loved me or my father more, certain I knew the answer: me. Instead, she bent down and looked me in the eye, hands gently on each shoulder. She explained that she couldn't help loving me and that the love of a mother for her baby was incredibly strong. But then she told me that the love she had for my daddy was a love of choice, which made it extra special. Of all the people in the world, she chose him and he chose her.

I would think about her declaration often in the coming years as my parents adjusted to my mom's new career outside the home and coped with raising a teenager. When my parents sometimes couldn't have a conversation without turning it into an argument, I suspect they, too, thought about their choices.

Now that I'm married, I consider each day what it takes to stay married—and in love—as long as my parents have. It's not that I don't believe in romance and the extravagant spontaneity of last-minute weekend trips or witty conversation over champagne brunches. But I believe more in the sacred of the ordinary. I believe in love that is sustained by deliberate kindness and the choice to see little acts as testaments of love and commitment rather than indicators of a spark that has died—of love communicated each time he cooks oatmeal and I schedule his dental appointment. This picture of love is certainly less exciting, but decidedly real, and in its own way more romantic because of the weight of its reality.

So, in the small silences of our predictable, boring day, I choose him, and I choose love, all over again.

JESSICA MERCER ZERR teaches composition and introductory linguistics at the University of North Dakota, Grand Forks, where she resides with her husband, Ryan, and sons, Eli and Caleb. After more than eight years—and two sons later—this is the love she continues to choose.

They Built a Family

LAURA J. K. CHAMBERLAIN

I watch from my window as they wander down the lane. He is eighty-seven. She is eighty-five. His name is William, but he goes by Bill. Her name is Agnes, and she insists on being called Agnes. Hand in hand they go, strolling together around the bend; sixty-five years of commitment walking side by side on a cool spring morning. Birds chirp. A squirrel scampers by as they stop in unison to discuss new growth on the sloping hillside.

He says he made a commitment to her the first moment he saw her. He was twelve. She was only ten—the new girl on the block. That's all it took, he says. At that moment certainty filled his being; he was certain of his life and his future and his destiny. He knew someday this was to be his bride.

It would be another six years before she secretly made her commitment to him. He looked so handsome that day; strong and like a man. His mother was crying; his father obviously proud. He said good-bye to them, promising to return. He paused for a moment at her front yard, then was gone.

She stayed devoted during those terrible months following Pearl Harbor when she could get no word. He stayed devoted while being out to sea for months at a time. She stayed devoted when the letters did not come. It was not until 1944, while he was home on leave, that they quietly slipped away to restate their commitment for each other before a Justice of the Peace. Two days later, he was back at sea and she went back to work at the factory. Another year apart, always thinking and hoping and praying for the other.

Finally the war was over and they could begin their life together, a life that has spanned six decades and seen four children, eleven grandchildren, and thirteen great-grandchildren. Fifty-one years of that life have been spent living in the same house, the one they struggled to buy during those postwar years when something called the "suburbs" was the newest thing for young families. The home where their children grew, where their grandchildren visited, is now where their great-grandchildren scamper over threadbare carpets, faded furniture, and worn tile. The home has seen many a storm, many a blizzard, and plenty of scorching heat, but it is still a home intact; a visual reminder of all the work, the fun, and the sacrifice two people gave to a marriage.

As holidays fill the home and birthdays bring children and grandchildren back from afar, these veterans of long love can always be caught looking at each other. It is a look of contentment and surety that goes deeper than love. A look that knows they stayed with it. And staying with it is why they can sit in their home today, surrounded by everything they love, quietly watching as their family unfolds before them.

Here they come strolling back again: my parents. They are still holding hands, still smiling, and still talking about the things only two people who have built a lifetime of love can know. I believe tender love has a power that cannot die and will somehow continue into eternity.

LAURA J. K. CHAMBERLAIN is a freelance writer for professional trade journals, and her first children's book, *The Story of Norman*, will be published in 2011. She also works for her husband, Dr. Kevin Dawson, in his Littleton, Colorado, dental practice. Together they have nine children and five grandchildren.

A New Kind of Love

RACHEL WEGNER

I believe love is not a big enough word. Nine months ago, my first child was born. The moment the doctor placed her on my chest and I smelled her scent, felt her skin next to mine, felt her heart beating against me, my heart broke. Every type of love I had ever known shattered into tiny pieces as the explosion of the feeling I felt holding her consumed me. Tears rolled down my cheeks—sweet, salted drops of a new kind of love.

I knew there would be a strong love. I had heard it was unlike any other, and I was ready to make room in my heart for my daughter. But I was not prepared for what actually happened. Suddenly, there was no other love in the world but that which I felt for my little girl. For the first days, there wasn't room for family, for friends, or even for my husband. She was there, filling up my core and flooding me with this new, intense feeling. Her hands, her feet, her skin, and those eyes: seven pounds and eleven ounces of—love. But that's not enough, that one word. How can four letters explain what I feel? It's a cop-out, a cheat, an absurdity to attribute my feelings for her to four simple letters. It simply does not fit.

Ever since the moment my heart first exploded nine months ago, it has worked on repairing itself. But every morning that we wake up with our bodies curled together and the first expression on her face is a huge grin full of cheeks just for me, my heart breaks all over again. Little pieces that pierce my very being, the result of a love so strong it hurts me inside.

I am a teacher, and I believe in my job and that what I do does make a difference in some small way. But this year, I do not have enough love to go around. At work, I ache to feel my daughter's arms holding on tight as I pick her up, to watch her smile light up as she discovers something new, and to hear her chatter about everything she is experiencing. I'm scared she'll suddenly stand on her own, take her first step, or say a new word, and I will miss it. And so I cannot be there for my students in the way that I should be and the way that they deserve.

Next year I will stay home with my little girl. I will watch her grow and develop her already determined and curious personality. And I will give all of my love to her, but my heart will still break. Because feeling her as a part of me, as a combination of the best things of my husband and me, and knowing that we created her and brought her into being, is too much to bear. But I believe that the shattering of my heart is the most intense and the most beautiful feeling I will ever experience, and for this, for my daughter, I believe that love is not a big enough word.

RACHEL WEGNER lives in San Diego, California, with her husband and daughter, teaching part-time for a continuing education program that serves at-risk young adults. She holds a BA in Spanish literature and an MA in English. When she's not teaching or writing, she can be found chasing waves at the beach with her daughter.

In My Father's Tears

LAWRENCE KESSENICH

My father and I disagreed vehemently about politics and religion in the late 1960s. He was a World War II veteran and a colonel in the Wisconsin National Guard. I was a long-haired student at the University of Wisconsin–Milwaukee, helping to organize antiwar demonstrations. He was a devout Catholic. I was an agnostic. My younger siblings remember all too vividly the violent arguments he and I would have. There was nowhere to hide from them in the small home where we lived. Once, my father ended up chasing me around the kitchen table, intent on hitting me for the first time in his life—and then he broke down crying.

The memory of those tears says more to me about who my father was than the memories of our arguments. He was a man who cared passionately—about the people he knew and loved, but also about people in need he didn't know at all. He taught me to care with the same intensity. I never doubted that he loved me, even in those moments when I felt least understood by him. And his life spoke eloquently about how much he cared for the less fortunate. He and my mother always did charitable work—preparing and serving meals for homeless people at St. Ben's parish in Milwaukee's inner city, for example—but after my father retired, he took his social action to a new level.

He was admitted to a lay ministry program sponsored by the Milwaukee Archdiocese, a program that introduced him to contemporary theology and the history of Catholic social action. This was heady stuff for a man who had never gone to college—one of the greatest regrets of his life, by the way. Suddenly, my conservative father sounded like someone from Dorothy Day's Catholic Worker Movement of the 1930s. He became incensed about how unconcerned the wealthy people in his suburban parish were about the plight of the less fortunate. When he graduated from the program, he became the social programs coordinator for his parish, and until he died at eighty-one, he was a thorn in the side of his fellow parishioners, continually exhorting them to give more to, and do more for, those in need.

It is in large part because of the example set by my father, Arthur Kessenich, that I believe I have a responsibility to give of myself—not just to those I know and love, but to those I would never know if I didn't seek them out: the poor, the disabled, the imprisoned. It is because of my father's example that I try to tithe, to give ten percent of my income to charity; that I spend two hours a week assisting a blind man; that I help lead Alternatives to Violence workshops in prisons. I don't do it out of guilt or fear of damnation, but out of love. Because I saw love in action, in my father's tears and in the way he lived his life. Because of him, I believe in love.

LAWRENCE KESSENICH was formerly an editor at Houghton Mifflin, where he encouraged W. P. Kinsella to write *Shoeless Joe*, the basis for the movie *Field of Dreams*. Mr. Kessenich now makes his living as a marketing writer while spending his free time writing poetry, essays, short stories, plays, and novels. He lives in Watertown, Massachusetts.

The Beauty of Aging

DEBI KNIGHT KENNEDY

A year ago or so I was walking on the beach and picked up a big, somewhat battered old seashell. I immediately thought of it as a Grandmother shell. I put it in my backpack and brought it home. As the weeks went by and summer turned to fall and fall turned to winter, I kept picking up that shell, turning it over and over. Running my hands and eyes over its contours, noticing its frailties, its strengths. And I kept pondering why it felt so good to me. It was soft and weathered. It was worn right through in places. The holes intrigued me.

On a recent snowy winter morning, as I sat quietly sipping my tea, I witnessed a lovely vision. There was the

Grandmother shell, sitting in its regular place on the windowsill, looking almost regal, I thought. Then through the steam of my tea I saw the soft, low, serene winter light shining through the holes in the shell. The wear, the tear, the thinning was allowing the light to shine through. It was a simple moment. A moment that is still with me. For in that moment, I came to understand why this shell had such great meaning to me.

The Grandmother shell was teaching me to appreciate the beauty of aging. Aging naturally, aging with grace, aging with all your wrinkles intact. I believe that there are lessons to learn that are just not available within the fullness of youth and all its glory. To be sure, youth is filled with its own unique lessons, not to be denied or belittled. But there is a certain humility, a humbling that comes with the wrinkles, the graying, the thinning hair, thickening waist, and sagging breasts.

I believe that Mother Nature knows what she is doing. As I see her softening the faces of my friends, my family, and myself, I am growing to love every wrinkle and every silver hair. I am coming to know that I don't know everything. I am beginning to listen. I am learning to laugh, a lot, with abandon. I am learning how to receive as well as to give. I am learning how to love myself—just the way I am.

When I was a young woman, the only love I understood came from outside of myself. It came in the form of a powerful need, along with the need to prove myself, the need to be heard and respected. Looking back, I can see that I was full of so many needs; there wasn't much room for anything else. Certainly not self-love. What I didn't know yet was that it is pretty darn hard to love someone who doesn't know how to love herself. I'm not really sure how I learned that lesson, but I suspect aging has something to do with it.

And now, with that little gem in my pocket, I am finally learning how to just be. Not do. Nothing to prove. Just be.

Now, I feel soft, a little worn. And with that humbling comes the possibility of allowing the light to shine through, now that I am able to let it in.

DEBI KNIGHT KENNEDY is a full-time artist and puppeteer with a passion for figurative sculpture. Life's crazy twists and turns have landed her in the beautiful and remote wilds of Haines, Alaska, where she lives with her husband and dog and near her daughters and granddaughter.

The Gift of Being

LORRAINE KELLY

When I left the jail this week after visiting clients, the soft breeze on an uncommonly cool May day carried with it the scent from a lone magnolia tree growing in a small patch of dirt surrounded by a fifteen-foot-high chain-link fence topped by razor wire. I did nothing to deserve that puff of cool air or beautiful smell, yet there it was. Just like grace, unmerited favor. Moments like that affirm my belief that to those whom much is given much is required. Jesus explained this principle in a parable to his disciples. Likewise, having been so gifted with the privilege of redemption, an education, and an abundance of energy and enthusiasm, I am privileged to be able to give of myself in service to others.

As a lawyer in the public defender's office for nearly nine years, I am enjoying a job that allows me to practice in real life, on a daily basis, the tenets of my faith. On those days when I am least inclined to go to the jail to see clients, when I make the effort to go there despite my worst impulses to run in the other direction, I am most buoyed up and filled with joy as a result of my contact with these troubled men and women. I always leave the jail or a meeting with a particularly challenging client with a sense of elation, joy overflowing. This despite the suffering, the terrible circumstances, and the bad choices that have brought me together with my wounded and hurting clients.

Many of my clients are emotionally arrested at the tender age of eight or younger; all they can see is that their current trouble has been caused by bad stuff that happened to them in the past. They are blind to any role they might have played in their own life or how they might navigate a change in its course. It is clear to me that, for the most part, the source of their bad choices and repeated misdeeds is love denied. I ask myself: Who didn't love them enough?

I believe that magnolia flowers are the most holy and amazingly scented blooms of all. But the harder you try to gather their perfume into your nostrils, the more elusive it becomes. This bears out my belief that the finest things in this world are fleeting, ephemeral. Mourning their absence only means that I'll miss their appearance the next time they come around. I believe that if I covet the past, either because of opportunities missed or grudges unrelinquished, I'll miss the good things of now.

Albert Einstein said, "There are two ways to live your life. One is as though nothing is a miracle. The other is as though everything is a miracle." I believe that the human capacity to love is the greatest miracle of all; it has the power to transform lives and create hope and light where there was only skepticism and darkness. I try to practice love every day, especially at my job, where daily I encounter people who perhaps rarely feel such love. I ask myself, "Is this a loving thing to do or to say?" Far more often than not, I find I've acted from self-interest rather than love. The gift of being requires that I learn and practice kindness and love toward others. The bounty of my blessings demands it.

After ten years in the public defender's office, LORRAINE KELLY was elected to serve as a county court judge in Pinellas County, Florida. Ms. Kelly, also a mom, enjoys spending time with her son, entertaining her very active cats, and participating in community service projects such as Homeless Court and Lawyers for Literacy.

Gray Hairs and Wrinkles

FABIOLA PIÑA

At fourteen, sitting on my parents' bed with my legs crossed, I looked at my mom as she frantically ran her fingers through her hair. All she could do was gaze into the mirror and sigh. She could not believe it. She could not believe that her hair was turning gray. She turned to me and said, "Fabiola, jalame este pelo, no?" ("Fabiola, please pull out this hair for me, no?") She desperately wanted me to pull out any traces of gray hairs, even though she was well aware that when she plucked one away, three would grow back in its place.

Then my dad walked through the door. He was home from work. As my usual way of greeting him, I jumped into the air and leaped into his arms. Even though he was sweaty, even though he was smelly, and even though he was dirty, I could not resist hugging my father; it was my daughterly duty. No, it was not really a duty, but more like the need of a daughter to share an embrace with her father.

Finally, I saw my mother and my father come together. In slow motion, there was another hug, another kiss. There, I sighed airily as they shared a moment that told me they still cared for each other, that nothing had changed from the first instant in which they fell in love. Then, as instinct, my mother faced the stove, turned on the burner, and let it preheat for tortillas. My dad sat down, taking off his hat—he always wore a hat to work. As he took it off, it revealed patches of lost hair and wrinkles painted with sweat. Then it hit me.

Each wrinkle my dad has on his face tells a story of hard work and endurance. In the same exact way, each gray hair my mom pretends is not there is a sign of wisdom. I know that part of that story and part of that wisdom is me. I am their child. I am their responsibility. I am a gray hair, and I am a wrinkle.

I love my parents and everything they have done for me. I cringe at the thought that someday I will have to live without them, but they have raised me well enough to live independently. Still, they are everything to me. They are my day. They are my night. They are my motivation. Even more, they are love, pain, discipline, patience, kindness, and beyond what any noun can label them as or what any adjective can describe them as. They are Francisco Piña and Maricela Marquez, and they are what I believe makes me, well, me.

Eighteen years ago, FABIOLA PIÑA's parents emigrated from Mexico to Chicago, Illinois, where Ms. Piña was born. This fall, she will be a first-generation college student, where she hopes to study Russian, Japanese, and American Sign Language to become an interpreter-translator.

Love Is Stronger Than Death

OPAL RUTH PRATER

I found the shirt hanging on the back of a chair in the cook shed when we came home from the funeral. It had been a beautiful day when he last wore it. We had cut the last of the corn, gathered pumpkins, and picked the last of the green beans. Then he took the kids down the ridge to pick apples, and the warmth of the day combined with the heat from his labor forced him to remove it.

There it hung on that old, straight-back chair, mocking me with its emptiness. With a cry, I snatched it up. It smelled of sunshine and fresh air, that wonderful outdoorsy scent of my husband emanating from this final source. I buried my head in it and cried, as I had been unable to cry before.

My children gathered around me, their small hands patting, trying to comfort me. These four beautiful children were now my only reason to go on, and from them I drew the strength to dry my tears.

My husband, Dusty, had had a heart condition, one that could be controlled with medication, the doctors told us. "He should live to be an old man." When he lay down in the yard that lovely fall day, he was only forty-one years old. Our idyllic mountain home became a lonely, haunted place.

Days passed slowly without Dusty there to laugh with me, read to me while I cooked supper, and rub my back until I fell asleep at night. When things got really rough, I would slip out to the cook shed, bury my face in his shirt, and cry out my sorrow and frustration. That was as close as I could get to the lost half of me.

Then the day came when we had to go out for groceries. It stormed while we were out and delayed our trip home, so we went to bed right after our return.

The next morning, I went out to the cook shed for a few moments of meditation before the children woke up. Some of our goats and sheep had taken shelter in the shed from the previous day's storm, and they had knocked Dusty's shirt off the chair and trampled it underfoot. I grabbed it up, but its wonderful, comforting smell was gone.

Fifteen years have passed since my husband's death. My children are grown, and I have to admit that they turned out pretty well. I still catch myself thinking, "We didn't do Half bad, did we, Honey?"

I heard someone say of a departed husband, "I loved him." How do you get to the point where you can speak of that love in the past tense? If that love is past, why does the memory still have such power to invoke both happiness and sadness?

I believe that as long as I am alive, Dusty's memory will live in me. I see his eyes peeking out at me from my grandson's face. I find something of his spirit in each of our children.

My husband's death affected our family greatly, but his life impacted it more. He will live as long as one of us is alive to remember and to love him.

And sometimes on a warm fall day, I catch that outdoorsy scent of fresh air and sunshine, and my face is buried in Dusty's shirt once more. Although I know he sleeps, I hear his shout of laughter somewhere just ahead, and I think he waits for me.

I believe that love is stronger than death.

OPAL RUTH PRATER and her late husband, Dusty, raised their four children on several hundred acres of land about three miles from the nearest blacktop, with no electricity or running water. Ms. Prater still lives among her beautiful southwest Virginia mountains, with her children and grandchildren close by.

Come to My Table

SHANNON LEE DENNEY

Every night at about six o'clock, I put dinner on the table. I know that I'm in the minority here, still eating dinner around the table with my family, but I'm used to the idea of being different. My family is different; we have four generations of women—all cooks—living under one, thankfully very big, roof. When you come to my house you'll find all five of us in the kitchen, from my grandmother who is ninety-five to my youngest, who just turned nine.

When you come and visit us for dinner, you'll come into the kitchen, too. You'll sit on a stool and be in everyone's way, and we will laugh and tell stories and cook. When the cooking is done, we will sit around the table and share it with you, because if you're in our house, you're family.

I believe in the power of food. I'm not talking about an obsession with food, but with the ability to prepare it. It's a powerful feeling to be able to make food for your family. It's a deep, nurturing, almost primal feeling. I think of Italian mothers who demand "Mangia," and Jewish mothers who worry their children, "Eat, eat!" Making my great-grandmother's chicken and dumplings or my grandmother's coconut pie connects my family to our past in a way that no frozen meal or take-out box ever could. I think of my family's stories from times when we were poor, but there was always food. My family grew it, canned it, preserved it, and served it on the table three times a day.

Why the urgency? Because mothers can't control the weather, we can't control accidents, we can't control those other people who are outside our families (and sometimes we can't even control our own families). When our children go out the door they carry our hearts with them, for they are our very hearts. We mothers can't protect them from every ill or evil that might befall them, try as we might.

But we can control what goes into the bodies of those we love. It's like saying, "Here, eat this beef stroganoff because I love you so much I want you to carry a part of my love in every cell of your body and in your mind as you remember the richness of the sauce and the time that

I spent preparing it the way that you like it because it is your favorite and I love you."

What do our children hear? "Mangia!" "Eat!" What are we saying? "I love you." And we pray that our babies will remember what it tasted like as well as how much they are loved.

When you come to my table, and I hope that you do, I will fix your favorite foods. Friends and family tell me that they've never had a bad meal here, and I hope it follows through to you. I pray that you will say, "This is what it's supposed to taste like." That means that you taste the love and care that I put into it. I prepare it with love, and you carry my love in the very cells of your body. That's power.

Although trained as an attorney, SHANNON LEE DENNEY's first love is cooking. She is a single mother of two daughters living in Milwaukee, Wisconsin. Ms. Denney began learning to cook at her mother's side when she was a child, and she is teaching her daughters to cook the same way.

My Best Friend

RAYMOND ALLINGER

I believe that my wife loves me. I often find myself wondering why, but she does.

Don't get me wrong. I do not have low self-esteem, and I am sure that I am a pretty decent man. But of all the improbabilities in life that I ponder, I spend a lot of time on this one.

Our relationship has been relatively easy. We do not argue much and we see eye to eye on most things, but our life together has been pretty difficult, to say the least.

We have been poor most of the time. I have had several failed business ventures and short-lived jobs. We have moved seven times in the last six years, and to this day I still compulsively make sure that there is a full case of ramen noodles, eight boxes of macaroni and cheese, and enough canned foods to last at least two weeks stocked in our cabinet. There have been many occasions when this reserve has actually kept us fed when funds were low.

After four years of marriage, Becky joined the army because she felt it would make our lives together more stable and, ironically, in many ways it has. We comfort ourselves in our frequent time spent apart with the knowledge that we have a warm place to stay and the strong likelihood of a paycheck within the next two weeks.

I was concerned when she joined the army that it might change her, which it has: she is more mature and more professional than she ever was. She is more devoted than ever to our family and, yes, she still loves me.

Our marriage is like a merry-go-round set in the middle of a roller coaster. We have never had a real honeymoon or vacation that I can think of; our financial situation never seems to allow it.

We are content just to be with each other, and we find our finest moments when our children are happy and playing or showing off their schoolwork. Sometimes we have fun trying to decipher our autistic son's special language that he has created for himself.

We are patient with each other, and we discuss everything from finances to child rearing in a calm, approachable way. Neither of us has ever had to say, "Honey, we need to talk," before approaching with a subject. We're married—of course we need to talk!

We live our lives as friends, work together as a team, and look at each other in amazement and fear when other marriages fail around us because the thought of us ever separating is terrifying to both of us. We respect each other and avoid taking each other for granted. Becky is my one, true, best friend. She accepts me for who I am and has never judged me for mistakes I have made.

There has not been much stability in our lives since we've been together, but amidst this uncertainty and unpredictability there is one and only one thing that I can say I never question—that is the undying belief in my heart that my wife loves me. And I love her, too.

Horticulturist and freelance writer RAYMOND ALLINGER lives in Tacoma, Washington, with his wife, Rebecca, who is a sergeant in the U.S. Army. They have four children and recently celebrated their tenth anniversary.

Leave the Light On

MARIANNE ROGOWSKI

Despite my desire to be "green," I believe in leaving the light on—the fluorescent kind, like the one that graces the ceiling of my parents' kitchen.

My mother told me the story of leaving the light on many times when I was growing up. It was, she said, a sign to her children that there was no mistake so bad that they couldn't come home. She was a devout Catholic, naive in her refusal to believe that her children would make irresponsible choices but realistic enough to convey the message that if they did get into trouble, they could always come home. There would certainly be consequences, but my mother would much rather have been the one to decide her children's fates than to leave them to chance. The light was a beacon for children who had lost their way and needed the safety of home again.

High school passed with my older brother receiving his share of late-night lectures, but I gave my parents little stress until I went off to college. In my junior year, after turning twenty, that changed in a most abrupt way. I drove home that Christmas Eve with my head sunk low, and I beheld the familiar glow of that fluorescent light through the kitchen window. As I walked into the house, my mother knew instantly that something was not right, and I looked terrified of what I was about to confess.

"I know you're going to hate me," I choked. "I'm pregnant."

Immediately her arms folded around me, and I released my long-held sobs into her shoulders. She rubbed my back and voiced what I already knew. "I could never hate you," she said. "I love you. It's going to be all right." My mother had revealed her light to me, and I finally understood.

Leaving the light on means unconditional love, the kind that you have for your children, because you are their last line of defense when life becomes too much to bear. It means being open and accepting of people even when, especially when, they're the least accepting of themselves. It's about the practice of understanding and empathy, not when it's easy to love, but when it's the most difficult. It's the kind of love that I did not fully understand until I became a parent myself.

My children, now eleven and nine years old, are quickly approaching the murky world of adolescence. And though I know it doesn't resonate for them yet, I have told them the story of the light in the kitchen. While I, too, would like to believe that they will never need to come home with their heads held low, I assure them that home is a place where love is a given, no matter what. When the world seems darkest, and they need it most, they will understand why I leave the light on.

MARIANNE ROGOWSKI lives in Huntersville, North Carolina, where she teaches language arts to sixth graders. In her free time, she cheers her kids on in sports, runs with her dog, Diesel, and is co-owner of two small businesses. The youngest of six children, Ms. Rogowski credits her loving family for fostering her belief in herself.

How We Love Our Enemies

‿つ

DAVID WALN

Forty-some years ago I started the fifth grade as the new kid in a small, rural school. The class had only eighteen students, but among them was an especially tall, athletic, handsome, and intelligent young man. At first glance, he was the person any new kid would hope to be friends with. But for whatever reason, on the first day of school, he had it in for one of the other kids and was using his status to marshal the support of much of the class to help in the effort.

I was a small kid and one of the youngest in class. But I was a "save the world" type, even at this young age. When I confronted this larger kid with my scathing assessment of his behavior, it went over like a lead balloon. You can probably imagine.

I had no idea of the things I was unleashing. On that day I became his enemy, and he became mine. It was an unfair fight on his home turf. I almost didn't survive the next three-and-a-half years.

Kids at that age have no perspective. A year seems like a lifetime. I could see no end to my misery. I even contemplated suicide a couple of times. But in spite of it all, it surprisingly taught me an essential lesson about love: Love is not about liking people; it is about seeing yourself in them.

So how did I learn this lesson? After the wounds of so much warring, that boy should have been the last person I would have wanted to empathize with. Honestly, it was purely an act of desperation. The conflict was physically so unequal, and mentally it was, at best, a draw. I had no choice but to try, in a very deep way, to figure out where he was coming from. This was not a short or easy process; in fact, it took years. But it did ultimately work out. Once I had spent enough time imagining what he was seeing, thinking, and feeling, a remarkable thing happened. I realized I had some insight into how not to make the situation worse. I even found a few ways to make things better. With time we both grew, and eventually we even gained each other's respect.

Could this be the wisdom of loving our enemies? Is seeing how you could be your enemy the key? I think it probably is.

I have been blessed with seeing the humanity of so many people at this point that I no longer doubt it in anyone. But I have also learned that the assumption of humanity—while better than the reverse—does little to resolve serious conflict.

There seems to be no substitute for the work of persistently imagining how I could be the other. This is what gives me the insight to actually change things. This, I believe, is how we are meant to love our enemies.

DAVID WALN is a potter from rural northeast Oregon. He studied art and ceramics at Eastern Oregon University in La Grande. He and his wife, Karen, have four adult children.

What We Tried to Do

LOUISE V. GRAY

I believe love is like pickled pig feet.

He was arrogant, stubborn, ambitious, opinionated, and absolutely irresistible because he adored me and loved me unconditionally—no strings attached—except a few threads like mandatory Sunday dinner at his mother's house, where he would drop off dirty clothes and pick up his clean laundry.

He was a writer who worked hard for $150 a week. He never whined or complained about money or that he was born with a painful disease called sickle cell. Yet his revolutionary spirit railed against the system that birthed bigots, poverty, and simple-minded religions. Yup, he was a handful, and I reveled in his passionate pursuits.

While planning an autumn wedding, my sweetheart told me that he expected me to be an obedient wife, to observe a six o'clock curfew, every day, and to make our home in his bachelor apartment decorated in red and white, his favorite colors. I gently protested. "But my favorite color is yellow. Can't we use yellow as an accent, like some pretty pillows?"

His quiet voice bellowed a resounding "No!" So, after some serious soul searching, I told him, "No, I will not marry you. Cancel the wedding!"

He was mad and sad. I was relieved and sad. We tried a few reunions, like one Thanksgiving when my sister cooked and he thanked her by refusing to help wash the dishes. Then there was a romantic weekend we spent full of oohs and aahs but still ending with the inevitable epitaph "nothing has changed." Finally, we went our separate ways. No Christmas cards, no birthdays, no phone calls.

Seven years later we had dinner and breakfast in bed and laughed at the foolishness of our younger mind-sets. But that was it. He later married and I moved on, resurrecting my filmmaking aspirations and dating occasionally. And yet I never stopped loving him and using his love like a battery booster whenever I needed to rev up my courage or soothe my sagging spirit. His love was unquestionable, persistent, everlasting. He taught me to never settle for less than "the light," that look in a man's eyes when he beholds me in both my peacock postures and in my most emotionally naked moments. My lover taught me that delight easily trumps any diamond-crusted bling.

Recently, I Googled my guy's name and found out that he died over a year ago—too late to send a sympathy card, too late to ask him what he put in his scrambled eggs that tasted so good, too late to thank him for loving me. Hey, I wonder if I sprinkle some red and white flowers in the Potomac River if he would get the message, that I don't regret what we tried to do, in the name of love.

Yes, love is like pickled pig feet: it tastes kind of strange, smells kind of funny, but when it tickles your tongue, the memory lasts forever.

A playwright and the founder of the Chocolate City Library, LOUISE V. GRAY enjoys collecting and recording life stories of ordinary people. She is learning to write lyrics for her family drama, *Greens . . . the Musical*. Ms. Gray lives in Washington, D.C.

The Most Powerful Medicine

ROSS HAYS

I have practiced medicine for about thirty years. In my daily work I see surgeries that can be done without leaving scars, medicines that have the power to erase memories, and lifesaving treatments that were unknown and unimaginable a few decades ago. Medicine has become a technological marvel. But not everything that is useful in medicine is new.

In my present position, working with seriously ill and dying children, I have, quite unexpectedly, discovered the most effective medical treatment in the world. It has no insurance billing code, creates no profit for the pharmaceutical industry, and, sadly, is mostly ignored in the medical school curriculum.

I am a professor, and I am a student. These days my teachers are the mothers and fathers of children who have died, children for whom the medical miracle was not enough. These parents carry the most excruciating wound that life can give. And yet they get up every day and tie their shoes and help keep the world revolving, caring for their remaining children, showing up at the office, and taking out the trash. Every day they teach me how to be a better doctor.

These parents—my teachers—taught me about this dramatically effective treatment. A young mother was deep in the suffocating pit of depression. One morning her pain was so great that she had no idea how she could possibly make it through the day. She needed so badly to be relieved of the suffering that she decided to end the pain forever, right there in her kitchen.

But then she reconsidered; she knew she couldn't leave her own father who cared so deeply for her. Her father and the slender thread of his affection saved her life that day.

A seven-year-old cancer patient was fidgeting and writhing with pain that was so fierce it would not submit to morphine. He gently began to relax and fall asleep when he listened to the soothing sound of his grandmother's voice and felt the touch of her smooth hand on his forehead.

A teenager in intensive care was being whipped and lashed by waves of fever, sepsis, and hypoxia, but he fought it all, refusing to be washed out to sea, until his estranged father arrived to say, "I'm sorry," and the boy could answer, "I know, it's okay." Only then could he peacefully let go and drift out into the ocean.

I have seen it again and again. I have seen it too many times to ignore it. I believe the most powerful medicine on earth is love.

DR. ROSS HAYS is a professor at the University of Washington School of Medicine and carries certification in three specialties: pediatrics, rehabilitation medicine, and hospice and palliative medicine. He is the medical director of the pediatric palliative care service at Seattle Children's Hospital.

The Value of Your Life

JENNA GREER

Five years ago, my mom was one of the roughly two million women in the United States to be diagnosed with breast cancer. My mom was also one of the many to experience, firsthand, the effects of chemotherapy and radiation.

She went through the expected symptoms: hair loss, fatigue, and general discomfort. The chemo was fighting the cancer, with my mom's body being the unfortunate bystander in the war.

My mom couldn't get comfortable anywhere. She would sleep on one couch, get uncomfortable, go sleep in her bed, get uncomfortable once again, and move to a different couch. My dad couldn't sleep in the bed with her because the extra heat he would generate kept her awake. This presented a problem: my dad loves my mother very much and didn't like the idea of her being where he couldn't watch over her. So he came up with a plan: he bought himself a mattress.

As my mom changed sleeping locations throughout the night, my dad picked up that little twin mattress and slept on it right beside her, just so he could be near her as she struggled through the war. Because of this, I think they both slept more soundly through the nights.

The idea behind a war is that sacrifices will be made to solve a greater problem. But a war without support is guaranteed defeat. Nobody can win on his or her own. Therefore, it is important to be thankful for those who stand by, through thick and thin. When the battle is over, as my dad once said, the value of your life is not measured by dollar signs, but rather by those who loved you.

Due to the treatments she endured and the efforts of her doctors, my mother's cancer has been in remission for over four years. She and my dad are back in their regular bed, though I'm sure my father is ready to resume the battle if duty calls again.

I am now in my third year of college, and soon I'll be done with school, ready to begin life as an adult. That's a scary thought. I will soon be encountering new wars, new battles to be fought. But there are two encouraging thoughts. The first is that my mom and my dad plan to be around for many more years to come. Their support and love has and is an invaluable asset to my life. The second is that I will be discovering new support and love in the friends I have yet to make. I also happen to know that there's a boy out there who will love me even if I kick him out of bed.

JENNA GREER lives in Fort Collins, Colorado. She is seeking a chemistry degree with a writing minor at Colorado State University and hopes to attend pharmacy school after graduation.

Hand-Knit Socks

DEBRA BRONOW

I believe in hand-knit socks.

There was a time when knitting was a necessity, and in many parts of the world it still is. Where I grew up, in remote north-western Alaska, it was more practical and expedient to knit a pair of mittens than it was to wait for mail-order gloves.

Today, in my warmer, more urban corner of the world, knitting is a luxurious addiction. It is a way to indulge my creative urges, support cottage industries all over the world, and even fit in some meditation.

Over the years, I have knit chemo hats and preemie hats; sweaters for adults and children of every size and shape; bibs and baby blankets; sturdy cotton dish-cloths and delicate linen hand towels. I presented both of my sons with hand-knit prayer shawls at their bar mitzvah services.

But always, there are socks in progress. As long as there are heels to be turned, I am patient with carpool lines, waiting rooms, and the longest traffic light in town. Socks are the perfect size to express personal style and practice new techniques. Stockinette or lace, toe up or top down, wool or cotton; hand-dyed and hand-painted, or a simple solid color—the possibilities are endless, and sock yarn is affordable.

Most hand-knit objects come with a long life expectancy and instant heirloom status. But that's just not the nature of socks. Hand-knit socks are made to be worn. Though they really are sturdier than the store-bought kind and can be mended, even the best socks will eventually wear out. People who wonder why I knit sweaters are utterly flabbergasted when they see me knitting socks; they feel obliged to point out it would be quicker and cheaper to buy a bag of those one-size-fits-all polypropylene tubes. Some knitters wonder why I would waste good wool and precious knitting time on a project that probably won't—and like underwear, really shouldn't—be handed down to the next generation.

To me hand-knit socks are a modern-day equivalent of biblical foot washing. Hand-knit socks say I love you enough to make something completely mundane but beautiful, with the full knowledge they will be hidden by your shoes. I love you enough to pay attention to the details—to the size and shape of your foot, your high arches or narrow heels, your preferences for thick or thin in your footwear. I love you enough to make something that, if used properly, will end up smelling like sweaty feet. I love you enough to make something that I fervently hope will wear out before you do, and I love you enough to stick around to knit the next pair.

It always comes back to love, doesn't it? Love and how we express it. Some people say it with roses. I say it with hand-knit socks.

Independent consultant DEBRA BRONOW works with nonprofit organizations and college-bound students. She has been a knitter, writer, and artist since early childhood. Ms. Bronow lives in Southern California with her husband, two sons, a standard poodle, two spinning wheels, countless knitting needles, miles of yarn, and several freshly sheared fleeces.

Deciding to Love Her

AMY SIMMONS FARBER

I believe we are marked by the people we love, whether we like it or not, for the rest of our short lives on earth. It's a part of the divine in us that we sense only when we pray or sit in stillness.

This discovery of love, particularly chosen love, came about after a long journey with my stepmother, Isabelle. I was thirteen when she married my father. Afterward he packed up my sisters and me and moved us into her elegant colonial across town.

Isabelle's house bore antiques and treasures from her aristocratic heritage—Persian rugs, Limoges china and crystal, oil portraits of her Confederate ancestors. When she became my stepmother, she was forty and nearly blind from the early onset of macular degeneration. Still, she cooked us wonderful dinners and made us say grace at the table. She washed my laundry and left it neatly folded outside my door. I even had my own room. But I stubbornly held back. The more I sensed she was trying to win us all over, the more I resented it. I corrected visitors when they mistakenly called Isabelle my mother. "I already have a mother," I would tell them.

A few years passed. Isabelle immersed herself in the tedious rituals of my high school life. She took me to the expensive dress store at the mall and bought my first prom dress— lime green taffeta. She hosted elegant lasagna dinners for my friends with her best china. She sat through every high school play I performed in, though her blindness prevented her from seeing anything. She always sent roses backstage. Somewhere in those years of homecoming dances, failed geometry classes, and endless teenage soap operas, I decided to love her.

Six years ago Isabelle woke up one morning, and the left side of her mouth drooped and sagged. Her smile was gone. A scan confirmed that the breast cancer she was desperately trying to fight had spread to her brain in fine speckles too small and vast to excise. Radiation bought enough time for her to attend my sister's May wedding. Then the long good-bye began. My sisters and I took turns to make sure she kept her food down and didn't fall out of bed. We drove her to church and discreetly held her portable oxygen tank in the pew. In the final days, we took turns reading her poetry as she lay in a rented hospital bed by the window, facing the ocean she loved.

The last time Isabelle spoke, I covered my hand over hers and said, "You saved my childhood. Have I ever told you that?"

"No," she answered. "But I am glad to hear it now."

One week after Isabelle died in September our adoption agency called to say that an infant baby girl was finally available. We named our daughter Isabelle after the grandmother who no doubt pulled some strings and made our long wait for a child shorter.

I do not have Isabelle in my blood, yet she is inside me somewhere, her voice saying my name, her small hands, her pleases and thank yous, all of her grace and good manners. These are not memories, but the being of her still around me, making me who I am—the mother I now am to a child I chose.

I believe that the best kind of grief for the dead is gratitude. And it's hard to tell the difference between the two when it comes to missing a mother who is now gone.

AMY SIMMONS FARBER lives on a horse farm in rural Maryland with her husband, Michael, their young daughter, Isabelle, and three Welsh Pembroke Corgi dogs. She is the communications director for a nonprofit group that represents the nation's community health centers. Ms. Farber was former Massachusetts congressman Joseph P. Kennedy's chief of staff and press secretary.

Love on Four Feet

SARAH CULP SEARLES

I believe love is steadfast.

My parents have a great big cat at home named Comet. We think he's at least part Maine coon—he has great big ears, a very large head, huge feet, and a laid-back, mellow personality—but we have no way of knowing for sure. He came from the local animal shelter. My brother and I didn't really want him, since he was a kitten and we wanted to adopt an adult cat because we thought the kittens would be more likely to find another home, but my little sister insisted.

We brought two cats home that day. Harry had the sniffles at the time, and Comet soon caught them. Unfortunately, where Harry quickly perked up after some medicine, Comet nearly died. He shrank to skin and bones; his fur was falling out, each of his ribs was clearly visible, and his eyes swelled almost shut. He was terrible to look at, and I was afraid to touch him. The poor thing desperately needed love and care, but I shied away from him.

Some years later, now a college student, I went home one afternoon after having had an emotional breakdown. My whole life was upside down; I could not go on without cutting some things out of my life, but the only things I could think to cut were the only things worth doing. I felt hollow, dead, an empty shell of a person. I had failed. I had no idea what pieces were even worth picking up again.

I found Comet curled up in a pile of laundry that afternoon. He'd been asleep, but he lifted his head and looked at me when I came in. Dully, I reached a hand toward him. He nuzzled it, immediately burst into a deep, loud purr, and gave me a perfectly content cat grin. I moved my hand down to scratch his back and sides, and he stretched luxuriously, lolling and showing off his belly to be rubbed, giving me looks of absolute adoration.

At that point, it hit me: this cat loved me. The cat I didn't want, the cat I couldn't bear to take care of when his life depended on it, loved me. And he always would love me. No matter how I failed, no matter what was going on in my life, no matter what I did, Comet would still nap in clean laundry, would still look up from that nap when I entered the room, would still love to be touched by me.

I believe love is steadfast. I believe that real love, whether it comes from God, a spouse, or a shelter cat, is offered unswervingly and unconditionally. Love doesn't consider past transgressions; love doesn't wait to make sure it will be returned; love isn't looking for something better and settling for less. We are all of us empty people, searching for meaning after our failures. Love is what enables us to pick up the pieces of our broken lives and go on, renewed, undeservedly but steadfastly.

SARAH CULP SEARLES is a high school librarian who believes curiosity, conversation, and a sense of play are key to what every educator is after: saving the world. She and her husband, Andy, recently adopted their first cat, Dora, from the local animal shelter. They make their home in Knoxville, Tennessee.

A Walk in the Woods Together

CINDY LOLLAR

When Greta and I celebrate our twentieth anniversary this year, I believe we'll do so as a married couple. Not in the legal sense—full marriage equality is probably a generation away—but in the best, most important sense of the word *marriage*.

When we met, Greta was an unacknowledged alcoholic and I was recovering from a near-fatal hiking accident. Well, it appeared to be an accident. I had tried to cross some mossy rocks at the top of a small waterfall and had fallen about thirty feet, badly breaking my leg. The friends who saved my life didn't know that despair had led me to look at those dangerous rocks and carelessly think, "Oh, what the hell."

None of them knew I was a lesbian. I barely knew it myself, if knowledge includes a kind of ownership. Now I recognize my homosexuality as a profound yet unremarkable aspect of my nature, like being right-handed or female, but back then I didn't know how I was going to make my way in a world that so violently wished I didn't exist. I was yielding to that violence when I stepped out on those rocks.

And then I met Greta. She was not my first love, but she is my great and lasting love. With Greta I have entered into marriage. When she endured the physical and emotional turbulence of addiction recovery so that she could be more engaged in our life together, she married me. When I confronted the inner demons that made me use words like *knives* in an argument, I claimed her as my spouse. We forgive each other, if not right away, then in the fullness of our mutual devotion. We laugh and play in utter intimacy. We hold each other's best self to the light, so that we are better daughters, sisters, citizens, and friends.

The feast of new love now more closely resembles a pot of chicken soup, but nothing is more nourishing through our daily rounds. We work and walk the dogs. We attend the celebrations and sorrows of our families and friends. She urges me into our garden when I need to renew my hope; I shine her beauty from my eyes when she doubts what there is to be seen.

Meanwhile, the soup is always on, simmering and fragrant. We are grateful. There is no thirst or hunger like that for lifelong love. Greta and I have pulled our chairs up to the marriage table, despite the lack of a formal invitation.

We are middle-aged now. Greta's back is bad, and I grind my teeth at night. Old age stands just over there, at the edge of our woods. But we will walk into those woods together, no matter what. I believe when we die, we will die married. For better or worse. What else could that possibly mean?

CINDY LOLLAR is a writer living in College Park, Maryland. Her essay was originally submitted in 2006. In August 2009, she and Greta were legally wed in Massachusetts. In 2010, they celebrated their twenty-fourth anniversary as a couple.

Sam's Valentine

KATHY HEFFERNAN

On Valentine's Day, my eleven-year-old son Sam begged me to allow him to buy his teacher an enormous red heart filled with delectable chocolates. We compromised, and he bought her a smaller but respectably sized heart. On his small budget, $4.99 was a huge investment, and I was touched by his generosity.

Sam has not always loved teachers. He doesn't yet admit that he likes school, but he does like to hang out in his classroom after three o'clock, and he is excited about some class projects.

Last year, Sam's most memorable achievement was having the longest "missing assignment" list in the entire fifth grade. He struggled all year to keep his head above the academic sea. Many nights Sam sank into tears of frustration while working his way through another pile of homework.

In defense of his fifth grade teacher, she didn't really assign two hours of homework each night. Sam was bringing home all of the work he had not finished in class each day. His focus was somewhere else when the other students were doing their class work. He may have traveled to Narnia or Middle Earth or Alagaesia. Wherever he was, it must have been much more interesting than fifth grade because he spent a lot of time there. Sam approached sixth grade with the anticipation of one awaiting a root canal.

I must admit I was concerned when I first met Mrs. Hogan. She was a beginning teacher. She seemed so young and sweet and inexperienced. How was this new teacher going to lift up a boy who had learned to dread school?

As the first weeks of school flew by, the same missing assignment issue reappeared. Then, slowly, it began to disappear. Sam had his assignment notebook filled in every day. Amazed, I wondered aloud which bribe had inspired him. "Mrs. Hogan checks everyone's notebook every day, Mom," Sam reported.

As I observed this teacher's interactions with my son at the end of each day, I realized that Sam's inattentiveness and disorganization were not the primary things that Mrs. Hogan noticed about him. She recognized Sam as a knowledgeable, capable student who loves to read. He rose to her expectations.

Sam began to do his homework without numerous reminders or a major search through his crowded backpack. He brought home less and less class work. He earned six A's on his second-quarter report card.

I still don't know how much of this miracle is due to the magic of maturity and how much is due to the magic of Mrs. Hogan. I do know that my son loves his sixth grade teacher, and I think there is a magic in relationships that can motivate children when nothing else will.

I believe that every child should have at least one teacher whom he absolutely loves and admires. Every child should have a teacher who inspires his best effort. Every child should have a teacher who inspires the purchase of a candy-filled heart on Valentine's Day.

KATHY HEFFERNAN and her husband are raising three children in Missoula, Montana. They have also helped raise three grown foster sons.

To Dwell in Possibility

PATRICIA W. BENNETT

Recounting how the 1930s farmhouse became her home, my friend Annie maintains that the pantry made her do it.

She'd been in the house barely three minutes and had already found herself smitten by possibilities: the beadboard porch walls; the dining room's built-in china closet; the living room's varnished French doors.

By the time she reached the kitchen, my pal, the Professional Woman, was starring in her own domestic reverie, imagining herself a 1935 matron, working at the pulldown ironing board, its off-duty presence betrayed only by a small, exquisite glass knob.

The seller's agent broke the spell: "You can always make the pantry a second bath." He nodded toward a golden oak door half hiding shelves laden with preserves.

Annie pictured the homey space gone: demolished and replaced with a standard-issue Mc-vanity and Mc-toilet from Home Depot.

"Another bath'd add ten thousand dollars to the place," the agent observed.

Annie snapped. "Not if I buy this house." Twenty minutes later, she did.

Annie and I go back as far as hopscotch and ogling boys, so it's not surprising that we both have come to believe the same thing about houses: houses, at least those with an ounce of integrity about them, have souls.

Houses, we think, get souls as people join themselves to a place and its possibilities; when a loved building becomes less the stuff of brick or wood and more the idea of belonging, of being rooted, of seeing in the house an extension of one's self.

My childhood home was a Victorian dowager of a place, whose size (eighteen rooms) and condition (deplorable) had underwhelmed every buyer until my father, a Marine Corps colonel who was fazed by absolutely nothing, bought it in an afternoon. My mother told him he was mad and was herself of the same mind-set toward Pop until she, too, fell under the spell of the place.

What was that exactly? I'm not sure. What defines a soul?

But that house sustained our hopes, sympathized with our woes, and was one with our family for twenty-four years until my father died and it had to be sold. Next to my father's death, losing 22 Inlet Terrace was the worst grief I've lived.

In houses like 22, there is a palpable sense of home: of welcome; of acceptance; of where, if you could go anywhere, you'd want to be.

We trust such dwellings, if we are fortunate enough to possess them, to nurture and shelter the dearest components of ourselves. Our children are introduced to the world by the sights from their windows, the aromas from their kitchens, the visitors to their porches.

We bring to the house our grandmother's favorite tablecloth, our father's handmade chairs, settle them in the linen closet or against the dining room wall, and feel the connectedness.

The house, then, becomes a habitation, not of one, but of many.

We mistake, today, thinking that the essence of a house is buyable, buildable, displayable.

No, the soul of a house emanates from abiding, of daring to dwell in a place, and in it, being ourselves, warts and all.

We breathe spirit, anima, into houses by living our lives, not maintaining a lifestyle.

I believe this: houses have souls, and once a house loves you, all things are possible.

PATRICIA W. BENNETT is an award-winning journalist and media historian whose writing often explores the concept of home and what she calls "inscape": the meaning we vest in the objects around us. She is currently at work on a blog and a compilation of her essays. She lives in Pennsylvania and Massachusetts.

Duck Blind Lessons

JAMES JOHNSON

The gasoline business led our family to Southwest Louisiana in the 1950s; the ducks kept us there. Rice country, flat and wet—duck haven. Our duck blind was a metal box, about five feet deep, buried flush in a rice field levee, smelly and usually a bit wet. I learned many lessons in this metal pit, hunting often with my father; the blind was our sanctuary. It was here that we were comfortable and where I learned. Dad was a big man, scary, a man of action. He was the boss. But we sat, patiently waiting, talking softly.

Hunting was simple for us—waders, army surplus coats, Duxbax hats, and Winchester pumps. No water, thermoses of coffee, or food. We went hunting, not picnicking. Waking at four o'clock in the morning, we'd drive the forty minutes to the edge of the marsh. No heater, no coat. Dad said we had to get ready for the cold. Gloves were not part of our clothing. "Who can shoot with gloves?" Discomfort was expected.

Hunting ducks seemed to consume Dad, but shooting ducks wasn't the only goal. Calling the ducks and working them over the decoys was his specialty. I remember countless times looking up at him as he worked a bunch of ducks. His green eyes were a little wild; his powerful neck was strained and enlarged with the effort. It might be cold and raining, but he frequently forgot to zip his coat. To Dad, the weather was peripheral. His warmth came from within.

Ducks were only to be shot in the air—no poaching, no dogs. We were a team.

The hunt I'll never forget was after I'd moved away. Dad was almost seventy, and I was home for a few days. I had a cast on my leg and couldn't get it wet. Dad carried me—all 195 pounds, plus cast, guns, and plenty of shells—all the way to the blind. "You're not too heavy, Jim."

I believe that I am the man I am today because of that relationship. I learned to do things simply, to stay with the things that work, to be patient, to appreciate silence. I learned that discomfort is transient. I learned that I was a welcome burden to my dad, that life without burden is a life without weight, a shallow life. I believe we need the encumbrance of challenge. As Dad plodded along through the water and over the levee, he occasionally stumbled, but never fell.

I learned to love my children in this same way. I have created my own refuge with each. Their weight is never too heavy. It is welcome. Sometimes I stumble, make mistakes, but I never fall.

My dad hunted regularly into his seventies. He never overslept; he never lost the joy of the hunt. He often hunted alone. In my mind, he's there now—sitting peacefully, watching, waiting, ready. A cold rain blows from the north. The mallards are flying.

JAMES JOHNSON grew up in South Louisiana. For the past thirty-five years he has been a professor at Smith College in Northampton, Massachusetts. He is an avid outdoorsman, but he does not hunt anymore.

First Friend

SUSAN SENATOR

My son Nat never had a friend until he was fifteen. He is autistic, and so something as complicated as friendship was beyond him for most of his life. When he was little, any social foray I made with him—be it a story hour, a trip to the beach, or a birthday party—was full of worry. I never knew if he would have a tantrum or completely withdraw from everyone.

Over time, I guess I gave up on the idea that he would figure out about friends. Yet I didn't want either of us to be a prisoner to autism, so I forced myself to get out there with him. Even though he had no idea what a friend was, he still needed to learn how to be with other kids.

When he was eleven, though, I discovered a Special Olympics gymnastics team in a nearby town. I wondered if this might be a way that he could be with other kids without the pressure of having to communicate. All he'd have to do is tumble and swing on gym equipment.

As I'd hoped, by the time he was fifteen, Nat had become very comfortable with the gymnastics class. And then D.J. joined the group. Like a stone thrown into a still pond, D.J. changed everything. He was Nat's age and had autism, too. But he was different from Nat; he liked everyone— D.J. was a chronic hugger. Boys, girls, moms—D.J. hugged everyone. When D.J. made his way over to Nat I tensed up, ready to intervene. How would Nat react to such an in-your-face kid? Most kids shied away from Nat because of his shyness and outbursts.

But to my surprise, Nat just stood there being hugged. No apparent discomfort at all. In fact, he seemed to like D.J.—his boldness, his clear, unabashed affection. D.J.'s mother and I laughed, just a little embarrassed at the sight of the two tall, gangly, teenage boys hugging. But as I watched them, something loosened up in my knotted gut. Then D.J.'s mom invited Nat to come over to play, like it was the most natural thing in the world, and I felt almost giddy with delight.

We got to D.J.'s house soon after lunch. D.J. rushed downstairs to hug Nat. Once again, Nat let himself be hugged, looking very smiley. They bounded upstairs together, and before I knew it, *Peter Pan* was on the television. I knew I could leave Nat there because he really seemed happy. I felt a confidence in him that was new to me. No longer hugging, the boys were sitting side by side on the couch, watching *Peter Pan*. Could I trust this? It seemed like I could. I walked back to my car, wondrously alone. I was shaky with excitement.

For the next two hours, my eyes were glued to my watch.

When I picked Nat up I asked him right away if he'd had a good time. He looked at me—something he rarely does—and said, "Yes." Loud and sure.

Five years later, I'm still in awe of that day. Because although I believe that true, loving friendship differs as much from person to person as snowflakes or fingerprints, I still wonder: why did it happen? What was the big secret? But I know there is no secret. Because after all, it was just two people, joyful in what they had in common, watching a movie, and hugging.

SUSAN SENATOR is the author of two books: *Making Peace with Autism* and *The Autism Mom's Survival Guide*. She is a journalist, public speaker, disability activist, adjunct professor of English and, most important of all, the mother of three wonderful boys, the oldest of whom has severe autism.

Amazing Grace

KORINTHIA KLEIN

My grandfather died twenty years ago. I was fifteen. He was kind, strong, fair, and very funny. When I was a young musician, he was my biggest fan. My grandpa used to applaud when I tuned, and I would roll my eyes and shrug off his enthusiasm as too biased. I played my violin for him when he visited, and he loved everything, but each time he had one request. "Could you play 'Amazing Grace'?" he asked, full of hope and with a twinkle in his eye, because he knew my answer was always, "I don't know that one!" We went through this routine at every major holiday, and I always figured I'd have time to learn it for him later.

About the time I entered high school and had switched to viola and started guitar, Grandpa got cancer. The last time I saw him alive was Thanksgiving weekend in 1985. My mom warned us when we turned onto the familiar street that Grandpa didn't look the same anymore and that we should prepare ourselves. For a moment I didn't recognize him. He looked so small among all the white sheets, and I had never thought of my grandpa as small in any sense. We had all gathered in Ohio for the holiday, and I'm sure we all knew we were there to say good-bye. I can see now that Grandpa held on long enough to see us each one more time. I remember how we ate in the dining room and laughed and talked while Grandpa rested in his hospital bed set up in the den. I wonder if it was sad for him to be alone with our voices and laughter. Knowing Grandpa, he was probably content.

The next morning I found my moment alone with him. I pulled out my guitar, tuned to his appreciative gaze, and finally played for him "Amazing Grace." I had worked on it for weeks, knowing it never mattered if I actually played it well and choosing not to believe as I played that it was my last concert for my biggest fan. The cancer had stolen his smile, but I saw joy in his eyes and he held my hand afterward, and I knew I had done something important.

I argued with people all through college about my music major. I was told by strangers that music wouldn't make me any money and it wasn't useful like being a doctor. But I know firsthand that with music I was able to give my grandpa something at a point when no one else could. Food didn't taste good, doctors couldn't help, and his body had betrayed him and left him helpless. But for a few minutes listening to me with my guitar, he seemed to find beauty and love and escape. At its best music is the highest expression of humanity's better nature, and I'm privileged to contribute to such a profound tradition.

So, this I believe: Love matters. Music matters. And in our best moments they are one and the same.

KORINTHIA KLEIN is a violin maker and mother of three in Milwaukee, Wisconsin. She blogs about her experiences parenting while being married to a soldier in the U.S. Army, and she runs her own violin store.

Love Lives through Them All

TANUJ BANSAL

I often reminisce about the visit by my American wife and her entire family—her parents and her sister—to India almost seven years ago. That visit, once again, proved my belief in the power of love, a power that can shatter generations of rooted prejudice and bring two extreme ends of the world together.

I was there to marry my wife, again, but this time Indian style. Six months before I was married in Michigan. Only two members from my side of the family were present—my eighteen-year-old niece and my fifteen-year-old nephew. My parents in India were not there.

They had simply refused to accept the fact that I was in love with a "White American."

Living in a small village in India, with exposure to America mainly through their black-and-white fourteen-inch television set, my parents—born when the British were still ruling their country—still harbor deep-seated beliefs and resentment toward those rulers—Anglophobia, as it's called. This belief is reinforced annually by Bollywood movies released around August 15, India's Independence Day, depicting the evil, broken-Hindi-speaking British general, or "gora."

So, we decided it would not be prudent to even try to invite my parents to our wedding in Michigan—a wedding they did not approve of. While my niece and nephew stayed with us for about two weeks, I was busy with the wedding plans and a new job I had started. My in-laws were the ones who entertained my niece and nephew. They took them to the Michigan Wolverine stadium. To a Tigers baseball game. To downtown Detroit.

And very quickly, these two kids saw what I had seen. People everywhere have all the same emotions. Parents love their children the same way. Mothers are just as protective. They do shed tears here. They do laugh loud enough to snort. Butter does indeed melt in their mouth—every time.

These emissaries went back and conveyed the message. And my parents warmed up at least slightly to my wife and in-laws.

We finally visited India for our Indian wedding. By all measures, it was a small wedding. My father invited only about a thousand people from around town. My father-in-law and I were dressed in suits, American style. My wife, my sister-in-law, and my mother-in-law all dressed in bright, Indian, traditional wedding clothes. This event occurred after we had been in India for about ten days, and my meat-and-potatoes kind of father-in-law was the only one who had not complained even once about the spiciness of Indian food, the humbleness of our residence, or the roughness of our travels. And when I saw his six-foot-one Polish frame leading a dance circle, clapping his hands to the loud and fast Indian music, with many of my relatives joining in and my parents looking on admiringly, that is when I knew—that after all, love had prevailed. Without ever being able to communicate with them fluidly, my parents, against all odds, had fallen in love with the Americans.

TANUJ BANSAL lives with his wife, Kimberly, and two children in Sammamish, Washington. His parents live in the small Indian town of Muzaffarnagar, where Mr. Bansal was born.

Brotherly Love

KATIE WEINER

I remember the week my brother was born. I packed a bunch of my favorite clothes into my Snoopy suitcase, grabbed my teddy bear, Snuggles, and stayed in my aunt's old room at my grandparents'. I went to the hospital that morning, June 13, having just turned three, and while I was eating pizza on a waiting room couch, my dad walked in and asked, "Katie, do you want to meet your little brother?"

Little did I know that I was about to meet the person I would give my whole heart to. I would do anything—help with homework, donate a kidney, take a bullet—just to make sure that he can live a life full of happiness. Although my brother may frustrate and annoy me, I believe that the love I have for him diffuses into other areas of my life, making me a better person.

One night while I was babysitting, my brother was outside and fell, hitting his head on a wire and knocking himself unconscious. Surprisingly, I didn't freak out—well, not that much anyway. Instead, I recruited the neighbors to help me carry my groggy brother up the driveway hill. I managed to maneuver him up the stairs, plop him on our couch, and, fearing he might slip into a coma, put on SpongeBob to make sure he wouldn't fall asleep. After frantically calling my mother, who luckily was on her way home, I kept a close eye on my patient. Even though it was only a minor concussion, I couldn't sleep until I heard the front door open and then the commotion of a tired little boy and aggravated mother indicating all was okay. Normally I shy away from blood or other bodily mishaps, but unwavering love for my brother allowed me to overcome these fears. In fact, it motivated me to become a lifeguard, a job I love, both for its proximity to the pool and the opportunity to help people.

I love my brother from a very deep place in my heart. It is almost a parental love. I feel very protective of my brother, and he feels the same for me. He once walked up to two boys who were bullying me and threatened to beat them up if they didn't stop messing with his big sister—an adorable action for a five-year-old. Not all siblings have the same symbiotic relationship my brother and I enjoy, and I am truly sad that those who have the opportunity for a rewarding relationship with a sibling do not fully exploit it for all it's worth. For if they do, they will find, as my brother and I have, that both will grow and prosper from the love that they share. Like moss to a tree, life is better knowing someone will always be there for you.

KATIE WEINER is a high school senior at Briarcliff High School in Briarcliff Manor, New York. She plays the bass clarinet, is a National Merit Scholar, and has won a total of four state championships in two different sports. As she prepares to leave for college, she is once again realizing the importance of her little brother in her life.

Old Love

JANE R. MARTIN

The young believe in young love, the Romeo and Juliet kind of love—it's all wild and impetuous, skyrockets and roller coaster rides. But, I believe in old love. I learned about it from my father.

At eighty-eight, Dad moved to Wilmington, Delaware, to be near me after living his life in New York City. I drove him to his interview at the retirement community where he would live. It had the same feel as the interview I went to when my daughter started preschool. My daughter's session covered sharing and getting along with others. My father's interview covered the same territory, but then the social worker mentioned his status as a single male with hair and a bit of money. "Now you know, Mrs. Martin, your father will be quite popular with the ladies. Trust me on this," she winked at me, "the casserole squad will be knocking on his door."

After I settled my father into his new apartment, I left him in his favorite chair with a cup of coffee. I felt the same way I felt the day I dropped my daughter off on her first day of school—a little guilty, a little worried, and a little weepy. Would he be okay? This would be the first time in his life he would live alone.

Two days later, he called me, the delight in his voice apparent, and bragged, "At the rate I'm going, I may never have to cook dinner for myself."

There was one lady, though, who conspicuously did not bring a casserole. He noticed her. She made him come to her, and he did. He said she wasn't like the other ones; she had spunk. About two weeks later, Dad called me and asked me to drive him to a restaurant in town. I said, "Do you want me to go to dinner with you?"

He said, "No, I just need a ride."

I showed up at the entrance to his building, and he was standing there with a woman. They were all dressed up. Instead of sitting with me in the front seat, he climbed into the back seat. When I stopped at a red light, I looked in the rearview mirror and saw my father's hand inch across the seat to take hers.

Over the weeks and months that followed, I watched two people in the late autumn of their lives fall in love with the same dizzying skyrockets and roller coaster rides as two teenagers. Old love has all of the same ups and downs, including possible family interference, but with a greater risk of loss. Old love is fragile, and time is merciless.

After four years together, spending every day together, eating their meals together, and traveling together, my father died suddenly when an aneurism burst in his abdomen.

It has been five years since my father's death. I loved watching him fall in love, be in love, and have a companion at that time of his life. I still see his friend, and she is now my friend. I learned from them that it is not easy to be old, and old hearts can break. I am in awe at how brave they were to risk falling in love with winter coming on.

When she is not working on her first novel, JANE R. MARTIN serves as an agent and marketer for a string quartet. Her loves are music, reading, desktop publishing, and her sheltie, Izzie. Ms. Martin lives in Wilmington, Delaware.

Pink Moments

CONNIE SPITTLER

Outside my window in Tucson, Arizona, the Catalina Mountains loom, great giants nine thousand feet high, hovering over my day-to-day existence. Millions of years ago, underground forces pushed through the earth. And now, these mountains stand, ageless as love. Often I lose myself in the beauty of the peaks that poke through the bottom of the clouds. Huge, dark shapes rise up and over tendrils of mist that wind through the vales like mountain music. I watch the Catalinas change as the seasons revolve, turning green, brown, and lavender.

When times are tough, I look to the Catalinas, seeking consolation. When my children have problems, I gaze endlessly into their shadows. When my eighty-eight-year-old mother had a stroke, I told the mountains. When my husband developed cancer, I found solace in the image of a cool place above the heat of the desert, offering a stability that eased my worry. One thing I've determined, it would take a lot of tears to wear down a mountain.

I believe that the Catalinas hold their own deep-colored magic. Just as life does. Once, in California, my husband and I visited Ojai, a town that celebrates something called "the Pink Moment." People stop and watch the sun's dying shafts light up the mountains, a quick, intense shading that happens when a high range runs east to west. I was told this custom of stopping everything at that first moment of sunset came from Himalayan inhabitants who'd found their way to Ojai. Reason enough for my husband and me to celebrate our own Shangri-La sunsets in Arizona. For only a few seconds, we connect to others in distant places, who watch as swatches of pink and rose wash the sides of eternal rock faces. And we honor this brief blessing, knowing it will fade in just a few breaths.

I'm a longtime student of "being in the moment" during sunsets. I grew up in South Dakota, and it was my job to wash the supper dishes, a chore I hated. That is, it was until I realized that most of the time the sun was setting just as I dropped my hands into the soapy water. Out the kitchen window the plains stretched on, lit with flaming colors. As I swished and scrubbed, I formed a special alliance with the rhythm of day's end. You can see my affinity with sunsets has lasted a lifetime.

Every day I try to remember to store up the beauty and strength that comes down to me from the mountains. One never knows about tomorrow. I seek to understand and appreciate the pink moments that shade my life from morning to night.

Georgia O'Keeffe once said, "It's my mountain. God told me if I painted it often enough, I could have it." And so I borrow her idea. It is my intention to own the Catalinas, keeping them ever fixed in my mind.

I believe in the power of my mountains to teach me strength and perseverance and give my life a needed perspective. I believe I will be in love with sunsets—and my mountains—forever.

CONNIE SPITTLER celebrates the importance of personal stories. After writing and producing videos, she now conducts workshops that encourage saving life's memories for others. Wife, mother, grandmother, essayist, Ms. Spittler finds renewal in the natural world that surrounds her, from Arizona to Nebraska.

Love Like a Child

MARY LINEBERGER

On our way to order take-out dinner one night, my seven-year-old son, Jadon, saw a man eating leftover chicken out of a garbage can. The man's hair and beard were long and tangled, and he smelled strongly of alcohol. When my son asked me why the man was eating out of a garbage can, I quietly explained that sometimes people are more fortunate than us, and sometimes people are much less fortunate. As we passed the man, my son asked boldly, "Why don't you have a home or a family?" The man simply said to my son, "I had a family and God wanted them home."

Jadon walked with me into the restaurant where we ordered our food. He ordered more than usual, almost doubling his meal. When we left the restaurant, he approached the man again and handed him his entire meal. He smiled at the man and also handed him his recently acquired tooth fairy money. He told the man that even though God wanted his family, it is okay to love again. At that moment, Jadon had no reason to love that man. But he loved him anyway.

When my daughter, Allura, started school, there was a girl in her class named Samantha. Other children picked on her or avoided her altogether, because her hair was never brushed, her clothes were always dirty, and she wore glasses that were taped on one side. My daughter was also afraid to play with her, but more because she was scared of the ridicule she would get from the other children. But one day, after we had gone through her closet to get rid of a lot of her clothes, Allura eagerly decided to also add some of her shoes to the bag. Then she found an extra hairbrush and some hair clips. She also added some dolls and books she decided she no longer needed. The next morning, she asked to bring this huge, overstuffed bag with us to school. We walked to her class, where Samantha was sitting, alone. Allura squatted down next to Samantha and explained that she didn't need the things in the bag. Samantha cried as my daughter hugged her and said, "Tomorrow, dress pretty so you'll feel pretty." Although none of the other kindergartners wanted to be Samantha's friend, my daughter loved her anyway.

When my children were babies and cried for hours over my shoulder and no amount of rocking would soothe them, they loved me anyway.

When my frustration overwhelmed me by their constant dependency and I had to put my children down and walk away, they loved me anyway.

When I heard the screams and the thumps of my children falling down thirteen carpeted stairs and I failed to catch them, they loved me anyway.

If we all took the time to love as innocently as a child, what would come of this world? If we took the time to give someone our favorite doll or our tooth fairy money, what difference would that make to another?

I believe that if we could all learn to love like a child, we would learn to love for a lifetime.

MARY LINEBERGER is a computer science student at the University of Washington and the proud mother of two children. She has a passion for writing and dreams of becoming an author. Ms. Lineberger was born with a heart defect, so she also believes every day is a blessing in which to live and love to the fullest.

A Death He Freely Accepted

GREG GATJANIS

All I believe about living a good and worthy life my father passed to me in one still moment.

On a July afternoon in 1983, my mother and I were out together when we got word that my father had collapsed. We rushed to the emergency room and found him lying on a stretcher, unconscious. He had suffered a massive stroke, and the doctors warned us there was very little time, if any.

I remember standing behind my mother as she placed her hand on his and leaned over him. "Tommy, can you hear me?" she asked several times and with no response. I glanced at a nurse, who just lowered her eyes. After several minutes, my mother whispered, "I love you, Tommy," and turned away, trembling and in tears.

I stood there alone beside my father. His pallid face was turned away from me. His half-closed eyes were fixed, and his lips were chalky and cracked. He was gone. And yet I had no emotion—no fear, no sadness, no grief, no anger—nothing, except one paralyzing thought—that every day my father told me he loved me, and I had never once said it to him. "It's too late," I murmured over and over. Finally, I leaned down and for the first time whispered in his ear, "I love you, Dad."

As I rose to turn away, my father stirred. He strained to turn his head, and his eyes wandered in search of mine. Slowly, he raised his arm and gently laid his hand on my cheek. He held it there and looked into my eyes. The silence between us seemed at once to be a confession, a forgiveness, and a blessing. Seconds later, his hand dropped as he fell into a coma. He died the next day.

Today, twenty-seven years later, I am still discovering the mystery and miracle of that moment. It is both my deepest heartbreak and my greatest blessing, and yet it still guides me in times of fear, sorrow, and uncertainty. In those last minutes, when he knew his fate, my father cared nothing for himself and wanted only to comfort me. In that final moment, my father passed to me all I believe about living a good and worthy life.

I believe faith, family, and service are the pillars of life. I believe all of life's virtues and miracles are rooted in sacrificial love. I believe in the redemptive power of forgiveness. I believe each of us is called to serve and inspire others through our good works. And I believe that with faith and humility we can discover that every tragedy and unbearable heartbreak holds the promise of a divine blessing.

Late at night, when I rock my infant son to sleep, I secretly hope to lead a life worthy of my father's last lesson. And when I lay my son down, I lean over him, touch his cheek, and whisper, "I love you, Tommy."

GREG GATJANIS lives in Alexandria, Virginia, with his wife and two young sons. His mother, Eloise, died on July 22, 2009, twenty-six years to the day after her husband.

The Blessings of Step

JANET JAYNE

For most of my life, I've been a step. I'm a stepdaughter. I'm a stepmother. I'm also a stepsister, though I've never lived with my stepsiblings.

Step relationships happen as a result of significant changes within families. Divorce. Death. But then, love transforms. Mom or Dad finds love again and we get—for better or worse—a stepparent in the deal. And they get us, for better or worse as well.

My stepfather got me when I was an incorrigible adolescent. He missed out on whatever cute/endearing phases I may have had and landed smack in the middle of my moody/surly teenage years. Our relationship survived because he loved my mother, and even though he had six children of his own, he loved my mother's children, too. His heart was, and is, big enough for all of us. Somehow, I had the good sense to meet him halfway.

It delights my mother that her beloved husband, to whom I am not officially related, is one of my favorite people on earth. My stepfather now lives in a nursing home. When I visit him, his caretakers say, "Oh, you must be Bruce's daughter!" I say, "Yes," and do not qualify; not stepdaughter, not stepfather. Our love for each other goes beyond the "step."

"Step" is how we describe a person we're related to because someone we're related to married him or her. But being a step is really about being a part of an ever-widening circle of connection. Families within families; layers are added as relationships grow and change. It is through this gift of overlapping layers of families—past, present, and future—that I believe in the blessings of "step."

Now I'm part of another stepfamily. The stepchildren that I acquired were already grown when I met and fell in love with their father over a decade ago. I didn't know the joys and difficulties of raising them, but our connection to one another forms another branch on my rambling family tree.

Of course, stepping is often complicated. Being a stepsomething sometimes feels more fragmented than familial. My two stepsons experienced the tensions of loyalties divided, and although their mother and my husband had been divorced for many years, my relationship with their father served as a catalyst. Lingering misunderstandings and unresolved anger bubbled up and burst forth. It was not fun. These are strains that many stepfamilies know well.

But I believe that successful step relationships are possible through the acknowledgment of mutual love. My stepchildren may not know me very well, but they know that I love their father, and they love their father, too. So I must be okay.

We recently celebrated my oldest stepson's wedding, where both the bride and the groom have four parents each—moms and dads and stepmoms and stepdads—and it took forever to get the family pictures taken. But as we all stood together, arms around one another and beaming, we formed another overlapping circle of love in a chaotic world.

I believe that we "steps" are lucky because we have so many people to call family. I have more people to love, and more people to love me. And in this world, we need all the love we can get, even when it comes in steps.

Although JANET JAYNE's beloved stepfather died before this book was published, he was known to carry a copy of her essay around in his pocket. Ms. Jayne now shares a home and a garden with her husband and an assortment of cherished pets in the Appalachian Mountains of southwestern Virginia.

Here's to You, Merrie

JORDYN MAEDA

This has been the most difficult topic I've ever had to write about. I have many beliefs, don't get me wrong, but they aren't exactly the positive, hopeful views on society most seem to have. I believe that money indirectly buys happiness. I believe that love is only a scientific concept romanticized. I believe that everything happens for a reason—but seldom ever the comforting reason people desperately search for. This is why I've never actually shared my beliefs. They aren't just different; by common opinion, they're wrong.

Regardless, I won't change my beliefs. Not out of spite or insecurity, but effortless complacency. I've never had a reason to change, because although my views aren't positive, they aren't quite cynical either. I've never had a reason to change, because I've learned so much from an unbiased standpoint. My beliefs have been the unyielding foundation of my life for as long as I'd like to recall, and I've never had a reason to change them. That is, until now. Until her.

I don't have a job. I don't have wealthy parents. I'm just an ordinary middle-class boy unlike so many of her admirers. I saved up for valentines, but all I could get her was a rose and a teddy from Build-a-Bear. I almost didn't give them to her out of embarrassment; she already had a bouquet of flowers, among other gifts, and when I did (give them to her, that is) they seemed incredibly cheap and insignificant. I wished her a happy Valentine's Day with a forced smile and was about to turn away when she wrapped her arms around my neck and kissed me quickly, then looked down, blushing. I held her close and kissed her back, which seemed like a good, romantic idea at the time—until we were interrupted by a teacher.

Being written up for PDA does have a way of ruining a moment, but that's beside the point—she kissed me. Me—a rose and a teddy beside so many elegant bouquets and expensive chocolates. Me—the poster boy for ordinary. I tried to find reason in this, but nothing more came to mind, except perhaps, love. And this was so much more than a scientific concept. No amount of observation and analysis could ever hope to describe these feelings.

Hasn't it become tradition to change for the one you love? And being with her has compelled me to do just that. I am happiest when I'm with her. Our time is free; I believe in priceless happiness. She's made me realize that love is something science can identify, but never quantify. I believe in romance. And finally, I believe some things don't have explanations, and we don't need them.

Here's to you, Merrie. I believe in love.

JORDYN MAEDA is a junior at Moanalua High School in Honolulu, Hawaii. He plays the trumpet in his school's symphonic band, marching band, and color guard. He is also in Moanalua's Pre-Law Society (mock trial) Team and in DECA (Delta Epsilon Chi).

God Knows about Sacrifice

~

LYNNE SCOTT

At age twenty-five, I said, "I do" to the vow of "in sickness and in health." I remember looking at my soon-to-be-husband, Darren, and thinking, "no problem." He had been a national champion wrestler in college and still was in prime athletic form. When he carried me over the threshold on our honeymoon, I had no idea that in twelve years, I'd be carrying him on my back up the stairs of our home.

One year after our wedding, Darren experienced massive leg cramps. Two years later, the ailment had a name: amyotrophic lateral sclerosis (ALS), Lou Gehrig's disease. There is no cure and no treatment. By the time Darren was diagnosed, he had already lived the average time that most people with ALS survive before they die. He lived ten years more before the disease literally took his breath away.

Unlike most ALS cases, Darren's was genetic, so we decided to not have children. At one point, a close family member suggested I leave him and find a healthy husband with whom to make a family.

How could I have left this man who charmed me with his corny jokes, great storytelling, and incomprehensibly bad taste in music? He took to heart the advice of an older friend, "There are two steps in marriage: step one, find out what Lynne wants, and step two, go get it for her." He gave me something no friend or family member can, and what I miss the most: cherishing.

I admit there were times I wanted to run away. Sometimes I felt trapped fixing his meals, keeping the house to his cleaner-than-my standards, and providing the majority of our income. I remember the day I wanted to drive headlong into an oncoming truck.

My husband couldn't run away from his body. He couldn't drive to find a truck's path. I stayed with Darren. We had made vows to each other before God. And we loved each other until death parted us one night as I was reading him to sleep.

During Darren's slow decline, we both questioned why, why us? At one point, I mentally grabbed God by the lapels and demanded an answer. I did not get an explanation. However, I got something more important. I realized that God had kept his vow to us: "I will never leave you, nor forsake you."

Before Darren's illness, I knew a lot of words about God. After my questioning, I finally understood the words and believed them. God is love, and love keeps promises. Love endures even the worst pains of life. It's too easy to abandon those in need. Deep sacrifices of unconditional love are the bedrock of human life. I've come to believe that through such love we can sacrifice everything, even life itself. And when I see the cross, it reminds me that God knows about sacrifice.

Keeping my vows to Darren was not heroic. Even as the disease ate away his physical body, his inner strength, faith, and humor shone brighter. Our years together, even the final painful days, weren't so much a sacrifice as much as they were the very proof of love's persistence. If I had abandoned Darren, I would have missed out on what death could not take from us. After all, love endures forever.

LYNNE SCOTT is a writer and operates a dog-boarding kennel in Alger, Ohio. She is the author of *Dingo Devotionals: Learning to Heel*, as well as two screenplays. Ms. Scott is currently at work on a novel.

Love Is a Verb

SARAH STADLER

Using the word *love* comes too easy. I know, I use it hundreds of times a day to describe anything: "I love this book," "I love chocolate," or even "I love summer." But love is so much more than that. How can loving minor things like chocolate and summer even compare with saying, "I love him" or "I love my wife"? The love that matters is the unfathomable adoration shown and received among you and people around you who care about you.

I once witnessed this kind of love when my family and I went on a two-week mission trip to an orphanage in Jamaica. The children living there were poor, uneducated, and abandoned, or separated from families who could not put food in their mouths.

After staying there for two weeks I was dirty and dehydrated. I wondered, "How can I ever live my life from this point forward and not be disgusted with the silly things I complain about when I have seen these unfortunate kids? I will never be the same."

I thought not having any running water and a constant food supply was horrible, but these children seemed happy even in the midst of all their pain. They didn't need TV, computers, good grades, and even perfect hygiene to look beautiful and have people look on them with love. They had an inner beauty that meant more than any of their physical features ever could. They knew they were loved, and in return they gave this love to me every day.

An eight-year-old girl whom I became very close to was sitting on my lap one day when she smiled at me and gave me a big hug and a kiss on the cheek. Later in the week she drew me a picture of Jesus and wrote "Love, Shanice" on it in big, yellow letters. Through her actions and the huge smile on her face, I could feel the love Shanice felt—the love she wanted to share with me.

I decided to thank the children for sharing their love with me by handing out toy stuffed lambs. The kids were all so thankful to have their own little lamb to love and hold. The girls were so excited that they posed with the lambs for pictures, and the boys hid a smile, trying not to show how much they liked them. After a few hours I saw the boys and girls playing together, pushing their lambs down the slide, and even buckling them into a red wagon.

I knew that I had shown love to these kids, and I felt better than any time I had just told someone I loved them, because I gave love away. I used love not as a noun or an adjective to describe my feelings, but as a verb.

I believe it's important to show love every day and receive it, because I believe love is more than a word; it's an action.

SARAH STADLER is a junior at Hampton High School in Allison Park, Pennsylvania. She is interested in pediatrics, and her goal is to travel the world, serving kids in need of medical aid. When not working at school, Ms. Stadler enjoys playing the flute and the oboe, volunteering, and hanging with her friends.

The Friend Who Makes
Me Complete

PENNY HAGIN

I am thirty. I have a child, a husband, and a dog. But also equally important, I have a best friend. I don't mean an acquaintance at work or a neighbor whom I really like, I mean an honest-to-goodness best friend. We have walked together almost every path of our adult lives: engagements, weddings, pregnancy, even the death of a parent. I have told her that her taste is sometimes bad; she has reminded me that I am negative and a defeatist. We have cried together, laughed together, mourned together, and continue to grow together (sometimes as much as fifty pounds each when we were 8½ months pregnant).

I view our friendship as a commitment to each other as well as a legacy to our children. When our families join together for dinner, outings at the zoo, or just playing in our backyard, the adults relax and commiserate about the suffering we endure raising two toddlers. Yet it's also an opportunity for our friendship to set an example for our children. We're showing them that the strength you gain in life will almost certainly come from a friend who holds you up (or holds you down when said toddler knocks you in the head with a plastic hammer). Granted, our toddlers are too busy throwing sand, biting, and kicking to notice, but we are laying the foundation.

I have tried so many times to put into words what I want my son to learn. I would like to leave a little instruction book or a cheat sheet on life. Be honest, loving, smart, caring, yet all of this can be summed up by just being a good friend. I want him to have friends that push him toward excellence and that hold the ladder of his success. I also want him to have friends with roots, friends who can call a spade a spade, who know when he needs to be grounded. Quite honestly, I want him to have a best friend.

I go back to my own best friend, who lovingly refers to me as "Funhater McNaysayer." My best friend, who is so slow that her twenty-one-month-old daughter already shouts, "Move, Mommy!" My best friend who refuses to buy anything that doesn't have what she calls "good texture" (translation: horribly uncomfortable jute pillows and sisal rugs).

But in all fairness, my best friend is the person who has dreams for me to be more than I can dream for myself, the one who pushes me to pass my own expectations. Some days she is my anchor in the storm, and other days just the storm, but her unconditional love and acceptance have made me challenge myself and chase a few rainbows, and this, I believe, has made me complete.

When not working for a hospice organization, PENNY HAGIN finds time to read, procrastinate on her true passion of becoming a writer, and entertain her friends with long-winded, descriptive stories. Raised in Louisiana, Ms. Hagin now lives in Fort Worth, Texas, with her husband, Joe, and two children, River and Lola.

A Magical Impact

JEREMY GREEN

My dad was the director of counseling at my high school. He was also a paranoid schizophrenic. He heard voices, saw visions, and suffered psychotic breaks that left him hospitalized for months at a time. He also had genius-level intelligence and excelled at everything he attempted, except a life free from mental illness.

He was a musical savant, entered college at fourteen, and received a doctorate in education. I watched him beat the U.S. ping-pong champion in an exhibition match, make impossible shots in eight ball, and without looking, swish a cross-court behind-the-back hook shot in front of the varsity basketball team as he walked out the door of the gym.

At pep rallies he would sit in with our world-class jazz band. During the last set, the entire band would leave the stage, leaving my dad to play a fifteen-minute drum solo, doing Gene Krupa, Buddy Rich, and Joe Morello riffs and inciting near riots in the gymnasium as my peers danced, shouted, and screamed as much as if Ginger Baker of Cream were the drummer, and not my dad.

In high school I visited him for the first time during one of his sojourns in the psychiatric ward of the VA hospital. Up to that point, my mother had always shielded me from what he became during his schizophrenic breaks. On the sixty-mile trip to see him, I realized that I had no idea what to expect. I was afraid he wouldn't recognize me. When I entered the ward, he immediately saw me. As I approached him he tried to talk, speaking rapidly in a schizophasic word salad. Though I couldn't understand what he was saying, I could see his face, radiating with the joy of seeing me, and I knew that even in his current state he could still love, and he loved me with overwhelming emotion. And I felt that love at that moment for perhaps the first time in my life.

As with many schizophrenics, he got better as the years passed. He bailed me out of many financial jams.

He worried about my unreliable automobiles. He celebrated his grandchildren. He called every Sunday. Ten years after his death I still recall the humor, intensity, and elegance of those conversations. He told wonderful jokes that years later I still tell. He would discourse on the beauty of language, on the beauty of certain words that weren't only words but stories of lives, like his own, that never quite found the path to their destination, words like *wistful*, *melancholy*, and *quixotic*.

I miss him. I miss those wonderful conversations that now, with regret, I was sometimes too "busy" to take. I will always be grateful that just before he died I was able to tell him how important he was to me, that he was always there when I needed him, that he never once let me down, that he was the best father I could imagine—in short, that I loved him as much as I knew he loved me.

At his funeral I was surprised at the number of people who went out of their way to speak to me about how my father, as a teacher and a counselor, had guided them, gave them a sense of purpose and self-confidence, and helped enable them to find a path that for each of them led to a fulfilling life. In hindsight, I really shouldn't have been surprised at all.

My father was a remarkable man. And because of him, I believe in unconditional love. I believe in looking past the surface and finding the uniqueness in each human being.

I believe in trying to live up to my dad's legacy by helping others believe in themselves. I learned these things from my dad, who despite his mental illness made a profound and magical impact on people's lives, especially my own.

JEREMY GREEN holds a PhD in counseling from Indiana State University. He is a single dad with twelve- and seventeen-year-old daughters and finds that the skills learned in his doctoral program frequently don't work as well as advertised. He is thinking about pursing another degree, in women's studies.

Put on Your Heavy Coat

~

ELLEN GRAF

I met and married my husband in China, then returned to America to wait for him to join me. The romance of our first year of long-distance marriage is epitomized by the letter that my husband wrote to me: "In my imagination I see your slim figure buffeted by icy gusts of wind, and I want to cross the street and stand next to you. I long to shield you from the cold. But I am across the world, not across the street. We must both be patient. I will come, and I will be with you forever. In the meantime, remember to put on your heavy coat. Please trust me. Marriage is a sacred thing."

At the time I did not ponder the fact that *marriage* and *sacred* were abstractions vulnerable to disparate interpretations. To these floating concepts we would add conflicting cultural frameworks, opposing genders, and individual eccentricities, until the perfectly balanced and neatly circled whirling of yin and yang developed a sporadic lurch.

What my husband liked most about our rural neighborhood was the abundance of garage sales. A neon wall clock, crystal punch cups, and glass end tables resting on gold chrome bullhorns took their places in our home. I kept looking away and then back again to see if maybe they were not as ugly as I had thought. Then he found a gigantic framed painting of the Swiss Alps on the curb and hung it in the bedroom. Once a day he took it outside, leaned it against a tree, and, sitting on a milk crate, observed it with pleasure through a cloud of cigarette smoke. Though I may have preferred empty space to clutter, my husband's genuine appreciation for shiny objects, careful brushstrokes, and sunlight on snowy peaks had more substance than my annoyance.

During this same honeymoon period, I accidentally vacuumed up my wedding ring and threw away the dust bag. Too late, I diagnosed the clatter as metal on metal! We carried on without that golden symbol of perfection. In the meantime, my husband disoriented me by not saying "hello" when he came in, "good-bye" when he went out, "good morning" when he got up, or "excuse me" when he bumped into me.

I in turn alarmed him—by talking too loudly, expressing too many opinions, and emoting, American style. Pointing to the word *ardent* in the dictionary, he stated, "You are very this word." He did not seem entirely displeased.

My husband never says "I love you." It is as if being named might endanger precious things. With few words, we share the implicit trust of mountain climbers, based only on the certainty that neither would purposely let the other fall. I have learned not to pine for daytime displays of affection, small talk, or random smiles—I have to feel the airwaves to know whether everything is okay or not okay. Usually I decide it is okay and go to bed, leaving my husband at the table with his ink and Chinese brushes or under the car with his wrenches. When he comes to bed, he holds me as if I might not live until morning.

At times I still feel my husband is "across the world," but in the meantime, and forever, I believe marriage is a sacred thing.

ELLEN GRAF lives in upstate New York with her husband, Zhong-hua Lu. Her first book, *The Natural Laws of Good Luck: A Memoir of an Unlikely Marriage,* was published in 2009. She is the recipient of a Ludwig Vogelstein grant for writing and a 2009 New York Foundation for the Arts Fellowship in Nonfiction.

God Is in Her Hand

❧

JOHN SAMUEL TIEMAN

When I was a young teacher, I used to baffle my students by asking them to prove that their hands exist.

And while my youth was in many ways both sophomoric and churlish, I take from those days the conclusion that the obvious is difficult to prove. Take God, for example. When I was young, I could touch God. The God of my youth was bland granite with eyes chiseled open and blind.

But first thing this morning, I found God in the indolence of darkness.

I can recite the Nicene Creed in Latin. I believe every word. But my credo fails to explain why I make no distinction between saying the "Hail Mary" and making love to my wife.

I use the terms *God* and *love* interchangeably. But these concepts I merely ponder. As for belief, I believe in acts of love. I believe that God asks me to fill the empty hand of the beggar. I believe that God poses the question every time I see the hand my student raises. I believe that I find God as I type the poem, the one I begin without knowing where it will end.

I can tell you what I believe. But I've reached an age where I don't care what I believe. Because I believe that love is not found in the mind or the heart. Love is found in the hands. Love is in the nightly back scratch I give my wife. My wife kneading the dough, that's love. Love is in the hand that crafts, sculpts, sews, caresses, soothes.

That's where God is. That's where God is the most obvious. In the hands. In my religion, Roman Catholicism, the hands of the priest are especially dedicated during his ordination. If I could, I would sanctify the hands of everyone. I would bless the hands of the nun who teaches the child to write. I would bless the hands of my wife as she e-mails a joke to me. I would sanctify the hands of the clarinetist as she plays the Mozart concerto. I would consecrate the hands of the carpenter who shaped our simple dinner table. I would bless the hands of our dinner guests.

I *do* believe in a love that sails the Caribbean in a honeymoon yacht. But just now, just this day at age fifty-five, this morning, I have come to believe in a love that begins when my wife gently awakens me. Because God is in her hand. In the hand that caresses my shoulder in the morning. The hand that encourages me, simply, to open my eyes.

JOHN SAMUEL TIEMAN is a widely published essayist and poet. His latest book of poetry is *A Concise Biography of Original Sin.* He teaches in the St. Louis public schools.

A Gift of Unique Beauty

CYNTHIA CHAUHAN

I live with several chronic health conditions, including long-term survival of kidney and breast cancers. Yet I remain an optimist who relishes the beauty of my life, even in its altered form. I don't have an easy answer for how I do this, but I do know that I am enriched and sustained by my current relationships and the memories of earlier relationships that fill my heart with love and hope.

Every Saturday evening when I was a child, we went to visit my cousins, bumping down the red dirt country road named after the money General Lee was said to have buried there. Beginning to smell Tante Lucille's biscuits even before the turn for her house, and eager to be hugged and kissed silly by her nine kids, my sister and I chorused, "Are we there yet?"

We always ate crusty baguettes at home. But at Tante Lucille's, we were treated to hot, soft biscuits as big as plates and as light as cotton balls. When our stomachs were full of flaky biscuits drenched in freshly churned butter, we'd sit out back under the stars, drink sweet tea from Mason jars, and listen to Henri and Beau pick their guitars and sing about love gone wrong. We didn't know we were building memories. We were just kids passing time while Mama and Tante Lucille visited.

My nunc, Pierre, was a good-hearted trickster, a trapper completely at home in the swamps of south Louisiana. Following his prey, he moved his family around the wetlands. I remember their house near Slidell. We had to drive around a bayou on a road that was more imaginative use of ruts than road. At the end were stacks of cages holding various sizes of alligators. Racks of muskrat pelts leaned against the house. My cousins poured helter-skelter out the door and ran alongside the car as we arrived. They greeted us by whirling us around and tumbling with us on the dirt driveway, all of us laughing with the pure joy of being alive and together. Exhausted by delight, we laid sprawled all over each other in the dirt. Then we laughed some more, just because.

Inside, standing at the stove, was sweet Tante Lucille, unruffled by all of life's demands and surprises. Her calm wrapped itself around her rambunctious children and restless husband in a cloud of love.

I believe the commune in community is what gives meaning and depth to my life. It is the people who I love and who love me who give me reason to continue when life seems too overwhelming, or I can't imagine having to face one more surgery or treatment. Then, I remember or am touched by someone I love, and it is all not only worthwhile, but it is also a gift.

As a little girl, I would sometimes go to work with my daddy. I'd stand rubbing my sleepy eyes while Mama dressed me in a starched pinafore and plaited my long blond hair. Then Daddy and I would cross Lake Pontchartrain in the pitch-dark predawn to memorable adventure. Once in New Orleans, Daddy strolled while I skipped and danced down Decatur Street to the Morning Call coffee stand for café au lait and beignets before he would start work. Small communings like these with my father or with Tante Lucille's family fill my heart with life-sustaining memories.

Each moment of life is a gift of unique beauty. Sometimes the gift is evident. Sometimes it is wrapped in weird paper, such as my cancer diagnoses. But it is always a gift.

CYNTHIA CHAUHAN lives in Wichita, Kansas, with her husband, two dogs, and three cats. She delights in gardening and traveling, creating acrylic and watercolor paintings, and writing poetry. Ms. Chauhan also volunteers with cancer researchers to help them develop clinical trials that are patient-sensitive.

Four Sisters in Life and Death

ELYNNE CHAPLIK-ALESKOW

I believe in Ivy. She was my youngest sister. She died in a plane crash with my father when she was sixteen.

Ivy was born an old soul. There was something in her brown eyes that touched your core when she looked at you. When she smiled, you knew that she understood.

I lived at home for most of Ivy's life. That was my good fortune. Our bedrooms were next to each other. We shared a common wall. Every night when we went to sleep I would call out to her through the wall, "Good night, love-love. Sweet dreams."

That was my nickname for her. "Love-love" described how I felt about her. It was a double love. We were thirteen years apart. She was my youngest sister and the daughter I would have wanted.

When Ivy was in high school, her English teacher wanted to promote her into Honors English. As was Ivy's style, she asked the family's advice, pondered it, and then came up with her own practical and clear decision.

On this issue she had decided to stay in regular-level English because she felt that her teacher was excellent. She said that when he spoke, he made her want to "hug a dictionary." Ivy was fourteen years old at the time of this particular insight.

She was the girl who befriended the underdog. If someone were made fun of by the group, Ivy would defend that person and protect his or her feelings. Her friends were a cross-section of many different types of people.

Ivy was quiet and gentle. Often she would observe others, not missing a thing. She was thoughtful, endearing, and loyal. She was her own person, her own young woman. Unknowingly she had no time to waste. She had only sixteen years to do what she was going to do.

Ivy observed that there were many people who were quietly giving of themselves but who were never noticed or acknowledged for their generosity of time and caring. After the plane crash, based on Ivy's philosophy, my family created the Ivy Lynn Chaplik Humanitarian Award at her high school.

Ivy's beauty lives on in her family's and friends' hearts. Each year in the hearts of the nominees for her award, her being is once again touched and her beliefs continue to inspire.

I have been blessed with three sisters: Linda, Susan, and Ivy. They are my treasures. They come from the same love from which I came. We are bound by DNA. Yet we are also connected by an invisible frame and foundation in which and upon which our lives have been shaped and implemented.

What happens when one of the four sisters goes away? Dies? Devastation and longing continue always. And then the magic happens. The unspoken focus among the three of us to keep our Ivy with us in life. If someone speaks of the three of us, in an almost naturally choreographed oneness, we answer, "Four. And she was the best."

There will always be four. We are four. We exist as four. We loved and love as four. We are four sisters in life and in death.

ELYNNE CHAPLIK-ALESKOW is founding general manager of WYCC-TV/PBS and Distinguished Professor Emeritus of Wright College in Chicago. Her nonfiction stories and essays are published in numerous anthologies and magazines. Her husband is her muse.

My Family Tree

∽

BRENDA HUFF

Reaching toward the sky, a tree's branches can only extend out as far as its root system. Like the complex underground network that nourishes all trunks, limbs, and leaves, I believe in a spiritual interconnection that ties all people to one human family tree.

When I was born in 1964, my chances of showing up on any official genealogy records were tenuous. Children like me, who were conceived out of wedlock, were considered "offshoots," best transplanted to another setting in order to avoid negative stigma. That was forty-six years ago, when young, single women were commonly sent away from home to nearby cities in their last trimester of pregnancy. My birth mother gave me up for adoption in hope that I would grow and thrive in an environment that she was not prepared to provide.

By good fortune, I was grafted onto another family tree, and along with two brothers I was raised by loving parents. Years later I also had a stepmother, a stepsister, and a half-brother. In my heart and by rich life experiences I am tethered to my wonderful adoptive kin. However, distinct Middle Eastern features have always set me apart. If the "apple doesn't fall far from the tree," it is obvious that ethnically, this apple dropped and then rolled.

When I was a child, every birthday I would lay awake at night and imagine my birth mother. I wondered if she was imagining me, too. When I was a young adult, I wondered if the person I was growing into resembled unknown relatives. My curiosity led me to actively look into my biological history. But mostly I just focused on "blooming where I was planted" rather than digging up the past.

My husband and I united our family trees in 1987. Together we have had the joy of welcoming the next generation.

I was so used to carrying a mysterious legacy that I was shocked when in 1994 scattered clues led to actually finding my birth mother, who had also been looking for me. This dream come true has brought connections to her and to her other grown children. Our similarities seem on the one hand common and on the other uncanny since we didn't come up together. Now we've had sixteen years to make shared memories.

Another one of life's sacred surprises was the opportunity to meet my Lebanese aunts on my paternal side. When we first met, our physical resemblance was so striking that we laughed out loud. The ancestral history I have learned from them is a treasure I am so glad to pass on to my own children.

At middle age I'm still stretching my branches because I'm deeply grounded in the love that has transformed strangers into family and friends throughout my life. Experience has taught me to have faith in the power of families in all the forms they take. I believe with each new relationship comes the potential to enhance our unique biographies, and our collective story as well. Rooted in a universal spirit, we are all part of the tree of life.

BRENDA HUFF is an educator who lives in Nashville, Tennessee. She wrote her essay in order to practice what she was preaching when implementing the *This I Believe* curriculum in her classroom.

Staying Close

GINNY TAYLOR

My husband and I had been married nearly twenty-two years when I acquired Stevens-Johnson syndrome, a disorder where my immune system responded to a virus by producing painful blisters all over my body. Although my long-term prognosis was good, I, who had been so fiercely independent, rapidly became utterly helpless.

My husband, Scott, stepped up to the plate, taking care of kids, running errands, and cooking dinners. He also became my personal caretaker, applying the cortisone to all of my blisters because my hands couldn't do the job. Needless to say, I was a seesaw of negative emotions, bouncing from embarrassment induced by my reflection in the mirror to humiliation induced by total reliance on someone other than myself.

At one point when I had mentally and physically hit bottom, I remember thinking that Scott must somehow love me more than I could ever love him. With my illness he had become the stronger one, and I the weaker one. And this disturbed me.

I recovered from my illness, but I couldn't seem to recover from the thought that I loved my husband less than he loved me. What kind of wife was I to even think this? Had I always assumed I would be the stronger, healthier one? Or did I just not know how to be a good patient? This seeming disparity in our love continued to irritate me for the year following my illness.

Then recently Scott and I went on a long bike ride. He's an experienced cyclist; I'm quite the novice. At one point with a strong headwind and sharp pain building in my tired legs, I really thought I couldn't go any further. Seeing me struggle, Scott pulled in front of me and yelled over his shoulder, "Stay close behind me." As I fell into the draft of his six-foot-three-inch frame, I discovered that my legs quit burning as my pedaling became easier, and I was able to catch my breath. My husband was pulling me along—again.

This is what I now believe: that love between two people is powerful, infinite, and so big that it can never be quantified into more or less. True love—not the sensationalized, watered-down media version—is forged by the fire of countless job changes, late nights with sick kids, days of trying to make ends meet, and years of trying to keep the romantic side of our love alive. I also now believe that during these and other tough times, love has the opportunity to become stronger when one partner learns to lean on the other.

I pray my husband will always be strong and healthy. But if he should ever become the struggling one, whether on a bike ride or with an illness, I trust I'll be ready to call out to him, "Stay close behind me—my turn to pull you along."

GINNY TAYLOR lives and writes in northeastern Ohio. She is the registrar at Hiram College and is working toward her MFA in creative nonfiction from Ashland University. Ms. Taylor and her husband have been building a marriage of love and trust one day, one bike ride at a time, for over twenty-seven years.

Love on Aisle Three

DAVID WUESCHER

I've often wondered about love. What is it really? I've heard love described as a state of mind, a feeling, or an action, but I was never completely satisfied by these definitions. Love always seemed to be something more. So, after years of not knowing, imagine my surprise when I finally got my answer, in, of all places, the supermarket.

The store was packed, and I was in a hurry. Four shoppers standing around a cart blocked my way. Thoroughly annoyed, I thought to myself, "My God! What's that all about?"

Suddenly my irritation disappeared, and I wasn't in a hurry anymore. The noise faded away, and I was no longer disturbed by those who blocked my way, for it was then I discovered what love really was. It was the baby in the basket they had gathered to admire in aisle three.

I believe real love is what surrounds every newborn. Real love is a phenomenon that can be seen by its effect—a phenomenon so powerful and complex, it acts as a catalyst for amazing, and sometimes miraculous, changes in human behavior and relationships. Real love projects a field much like the invisible lines of force surrounding a magnet. In this case real love was about four feet in diameter, globe-shaped, and floated about three feet off the floor. Though invisible to the naked eye, there was no way to miss it.

I saw people busy with their shopping suddenly stop, transfixed by what surrounded that baby. They experienced what had to be some kind of vision. I believe each of them got to briefly see themselves as commonly bound together with a common birthright, so much more alike than different. The effect was so attractive I felt compelled to follow as real love rolled down the aisle and serenely turned the corner. I hurried to catch up.

Real love worked its magic on all who came near. Reasonable adults began speaking in tongues, cooing and clucking, oohing and aahing. Perfect strangers began exchanging intimate information. There was affectionate touching and laughter. Yet no one passed judgment or took offense at such curious behavior among strangers. Instead there were expressions of delight coupled with shared hopes, and a dream or two. There were smiles all around.

As each person resumed his or her shopping and left real love behind, the laughter stopped and we all returned to our mundane chores. The last I saw of real love that day, it was being strapped into the backseat of an SUV.

Now when I shop I remember how important it is for me to spend some time in what surrounds those babies. I take a moment from my busy schedule to coo and cluck, to converse with complete strangers as if they were long-lost friends. And perhaps they are. Perhaps we have all lost our way a little, lost our ability to see the real love that surrounds each of us. Neither intruding nor demanding, judging not, I believe real love serves but one purpose—to remind me that I am a facet on the face of its crystal vision, and when I stop to stand with my fellows in the sunlight of its spirit, we all shine.

DAVID WUESCHER was born and raised in New Orleans. He graduated from Tulane University and served in Vietnam as an interrogations officer with the 101st Airborne. He now resides in Los Angeles, California, where he is a certified senior fitness instructor and, when he's not busy training clients, he enjoys paragliding as often as he can.

Swing-Shift Kisses

∽

SCOTT SAALMAN

My mother and father kiss, she inside the house, he outside; their lips touch through the door's opening. The kiss is sweet and sincere, something to look forward to, though it marks the moment of his leaving and her staying, the tearing of their togetherness, the inseparables separated.

Sprawled on the living room floor, I take a time-out from my spirited reenactments of wrestling matches televised from Evansville. I scrawl names of wrestlers on slips of paper—Jackie Fargo, Jerry Lawler, Tojo Yamamoto—and blindly draw them from Tupperware. I become the names drawn, acting out their parts in make-believe, bloody bouts; slamming into imaginary turnbuckles; elbow-smashing air; headlocking a pillow. The wrestling, my restlessness, pauses for their doorway kiss.

My father is a swing-shift man, so the time the kiss occurs varies. One week he works 8 a.m. to 4 p.m., so the kiss happens at 7:15 a.m. The next week he works 4 p.m. to midnight; at 3:15 p.m., they kiss. I can only imagine the following week's midnight shift (12 a.m. to 8 a.m.) kiss. Perhaps at 11:15 p.m. he brushes back her hair and targets her sleeping forehead.

The house smells of fried eggs and Folgers, a swing-shift man's fuel and farewell scent. His face on a badge is clipped to his shirt pocket that holds his safety glasses. His short-sleeved, button-down shirt is tucked into his jeans. He leans inside toward my tiptoed mother. I spy this day-shift kiss, this connection of reassurance.

He straightens from the pucker. He holds a black lunch box, which holds an egg sandwich, six wheat and cheese crackers, and black coffee in a checkerboard-colored plastic thermos. He wears steel-toed boots, the bottom's a mix of machine-shop grime and metal shavings. His boots aren't allowed on her carpet. My mother wears fuzzy socks, so worn in back from her household laps that you can see the pink of heels, rosebuds of a dutiful housewife.

"Call me," she says, like clockwork. There are bridge tickets to buy, a river to cross. An aluminum plant awaits him.

I'm forty-five now, yet I replay the kiss often. Though it lasted barely an eye-blink in real time, it is a timeless kiss. My parents still maintain a solid marriage. It's a tough act to follow. I've made missteps in the minefields of love, but the reassurance represented by this remembered kiss always returns. I still believe in that kiss. I still try.

"I'll call," he says. At the end of the driveway, he stops his pickup. He looks for her in the rearview mirror, sees her reflection, and waves. The back of his right hand waves slowly, right-to-left, left-to-right, like windshield wipers on low, and she reacts with a full-armed wave, the kind one expects at parades. He drives away.

The sliding door closes, my bouts begin.

SCOTT SAALMAN is director of employee communications for Kimball International, Inc. He resides, writes, plays Scrabble, and is a parent in Jasper, Indiana. His parents, M.J. and Patricia, are currently enjoying their forty-seventh year of marriage.

The Courage to Let Go

GALE A. WORKMAN

I spent the last twenty-seven hours of my mother's life sitting by her hospital bed. Mom's oxygen-assisted breathing beat the rhythm to her dance toward heaven. Three weeks earlier, Mom told Daddy she wanted to go to heaven. She was nearly there.

The past year had been a misery: two broken hips, a broken wrist, a dislocated collarbone, dementia, hospitals, nursing homes, wheelchairs, and walkers. A potty chair replaced the nightstand between Mom's and Daddy's beds. The worst was when Mom no longer recognized her husband of fifty-one years.

"How did we meet that man?" Mom whispered to me, cutting her eyes toward Daddy.

Later, Mom refused to eat ice cream because she said "that man" was poisoning her.

Each time I watched Daddy answer the bell Mom rang dozens of times daily, I choked back sobs. He loved her so.

"What do you need, sweetie?" he asked tenderly, patting her forearm. Then he'd lift her from the bed to her recliner. "You're so beautiful, sweetheart. I love you," he'd coo, and he'd kiss her forehead.

I was with Daddy and Mom when the doctor said pneumonia was winning the battle. Mom was unconscious. Daddy decided it was time to let Mom go to heaven. The hospice sent two angels in nursing uniforms to guide us as Mom found her way. They took care of the business of dying while Daddy and I sat, holding Mom's hands, watching the clock, and waiting for the pharmacist's comfort cocktail to arrive.

That night, I sat alone with Mom. The nurse stopped in to check on her morphine drip, and I asked him if Mom seemed comfortable. "Oh, yes," he smiled. "Talk to her. Tell her it's okay to go. Then, she'll finish her journey."

When Mom and I were alone again, I talked to her. "Bye, Mom. I'll miss you. Don't worry about me. You did a great job raising me. I'll watch over Daddy. I love you, Mom."

Three hours later, Daddy and I watched as Mom drew her last breath. I held her hand. Daddy hugged her.

"Remember what I told you, honey," he whispered. "You get a place ready for me. I love you."

In losing Mom, I found a deep respect for Daddy. I am awed by the love and courage he demonstrated in the last year of Mom's life. Caregiving is the hardest job, yet Daddy did it with a strength and grace that allowed Mom to live and die with dignity. Seeing his commitment to her—even when the work left him exhausted and despairing—deepened my love for Daddy, and for them as a couple.

I believe it was finding comfort in Daddy's daily demonstrations of love that gave me the courage to let Mom go.

GALE A. WORKMAN is a journalism professor in Tallahassee, Florida. She worked as a reporter and editor for five daily newspapers and two television stations. Her father, eighty-eight, lives independently in Melbourne, Florida, in the home he and his wife shared for nearly twenty years.

All the Mothering You Do

⸎

PATRICE VECCHIONE

On Mother's Day my husband handed me a hastily wrapped box. Its shape didn't give the gift away. But more than the packaging, it was the gift's timing that confused me. There was nothing about Mother's Day that warranted a present coming my way—I'm a childless woman. And if my husband hadn't walked into the crowded room the afternoon he did, when I was thirty-seven, I'd likely be a middle-aged, unmarried woman, too. I was certain that I'd die single, and I wasn't too miffed about it either. Before meeting Michael, men came into my life and were gone— either because I asked them to go or because they got a true sense of me—before their yesterday's towels could dry on the line.

I'm not easy to live with. Being a writer and artist, I don't have a steady paycheck, nor do I earn a lot of money. Teaching has me home sometimes and traveling others. My moods fluctuate more than northern California's summer weather. Because my true master is art, this heart cracks open at the least provocation and tears make a river of my life. I can't stand loud music, must eat dinner before eight, find social behavior difficult to conform to, crave abundant reassurance, need to be alone often and for days at a time, have a temper that flares like a match, write about my most intimate moments and then proceed to publish and read those poems and stories to audiences. See what I mean?

When Michael walked into my life he seemed damn close to perfect. He was kind. He had a job. His car worked. He was good to his mother. And the man pays attention—he knows just when my mood dips below sea level and asks what's wrong and listens to the answer, rarely looking skyward as he does. He doesn't bring me flowers unless they're straight from his father's garden. He leaves his socks on the living room floor to remind me of how well rounded he is. He comes home close to when he says he will, never says anything mean, and rarely raises his voice. So what if the bathtub doesn't get cleaned every week?

When I opened that box on Mother's Day, there was a double strand of freshwater pearls inside. "For all the mothering you do, all those kids you teach, and the grown-ups, too," Michael said.

For me, the question isn't *what* I believe in, it's who. I believe in my husband. I believe in love.

PATRICE VECCHIONE is the author of *Writing and the Spiritual Life: Finding Your Voice by Looking Within* and a collection of poems, *Territory of Wind*. She is also the editor of many poetry anthologies for young people, including *Faith and Doubt*.

Life Is a Battle

ELLIANA GRACE

I believe in the healing power of love. I believe in love's ability to transform and mend a broken life. I believe that we're called to love one another, beyond ourselves, with a love that only comes from above. As Gandhi once said, "Where there is love there is life."

I've spent a majority of my life feeling like I'm unlovable. Rarely would my parents hold me or tell me that they loved me, and through this I perceived their behavior as a lack of love for me. The weight of feeling worthless fell heavier on me with each passing day, and I began to search for anything to take that pain away. Countless nights I'd stay up alone in my room, trying to understand what I might have done to not deserve their love. An overwhelming self-hatred took over my mind and spilled over into my actions. However, I didn't want anyone to know how badly I was hurting because I didn't want to be rejected. In the presence of others, I learned to carry myself happily. But when I was alone I could no longer pretend. Often I would wait until everyone was asleep and I could take a few pills to relax. Many times I just wouldn't come home at all. My nightly behavior took over my days, as well, and I became addicted to various drugs to get me through. The hatred I had for myself grew, and I couldn't stand to be in my own skin.

In the midst of this, a married couple that taught at my high school began to spend time with me. They spent time with me daily. They were fully aware of my drug addiction and watched as each day I detached myself a little bit more from life. Never once did they try to change me; they simply loved me, in spite of myself. No one had ever done that before. At first it irritated me. I didn't understand it; however, they still loved me. After a while, I told them of my plans to end my life. I told them that I didn't want to do it, but I felt that I had no choice. They didn't judge, nor did they plead with me to reconsider. Instead, they loved me unconditionally and truly listened to all of the thoughts that no one prior had taken the time to ask about. As theologian Paul Tillich has said, "The first duty of love is to listen." This couple took time daily to listen to me and through that taught me what love truly is.

It has been five years since I originally met this couple. I've been drug free for two and a half years now, and I'm loving life more than I ever imagined possible. Life is a battle, but it is worth the fight. I believe that love offers redemption that heals. And I believe that love truly has the power to transform a broken heart and give it life.

ELLIANA GRACE is studying counseling at Liberty University. Her desire is to work with troubled adolescents. In addition to writing, she enjoys music, reading, and spending time with loved ones.

I Believe in You

JULIE CHINITZ

Okay, here it is: I believe in the power of love.

I was a college student the first time I fell in love. I was spending a summer in Seattle, taking an extra class and washing dishes for money. My kitchen manager asked me to interpret a message into Spanish for one of the other dishwashers. I did not expect that that would be the day I'd fall in love, but it was. When I met Daniel, it washed over me. That's the way love is, I learned. It inhabits you entirely.

One year later, I finished college and arrived at Daniel's apartment with an enormous suitcase. One more year after that, I returned back east for a short summer and worked for an attorney who had made a name for himself in international human rights circles.

"Do you want to do important things in your life?" the attorney asked me.

I told him I thought I did.

"How are you going to do that with a Mexican man twice your age?" he wondered. To that he could have added undocumented, divorced with two children, and more or less penniless.

I said, "I guess it depends on what you consider important."

Then I returned to Seattle, to Daniel, and soon after learned one of the many remarkable things he would teach me. It happened when I inadvertently passed along a story he had told me in confidence. Because I also believe in honesty, I confessed.

Looking back now, I don't remember the confidence, but I do remember Daniel's response. "I can't get angry with you, because you didn't mean to hurt me," he said. "You just made a mistake."

From me, Daniel learned how to argue, realizing that it can be beautiful rather than ugly. He also found freedom to laugh, tease, and be silly.

After living together for a year and half, I made Daniel marry me, not because I believe in rituals, but because he needed his green card and I needed him to have it. Three years after that he let me leave him, since I had been too young when we met, and then he let me return home once I was old enough, no questions asked.

Soon we will have known each other for fourteen years. The love dwells even deeper within me. A couple of years ago, I was traveling abroad for work and had a disagreement with my supervisor, a silly dispute but one that tested my sense of pride. Standing on a cobblestone street in Oaxaca, Mexico, I called Daniel and told him that I might have to quit my job. He did not ask for any details, saying only, "Don't worry. I support you."

Someday, I want to find that street again, and that pay phone. I will show it to Daniel and tell him, "If I can believe in only one thing, I believe in you."

ATTORNEY JULIE CHINITZ works in the field of community organizing. She recently coedited *An American Debt Unpaid: Stories of Native Health.* Ms. Chinitz lives with her husband, Daniel, in Seattle and Philadelphia.

Show and Tell

ANN ERIK

My mom has never told me she loves me. That doesn't mean she doesn't, of course—she just has a different way of expressing it.

When I was thirteen and growing up in Estonia, I fell from the top of a haystack. We had been working in the fields of the countryside where my grandma lived. And like hundreds of times before, after all the hay was gathered, I climbed on the top of the haystack on my uncle's truck for a fun ride home. But the fun ride didn't last long; it ended with two fractured wrists and a cut right knee.

My mom picked me up and carried me to the house. She made a cast out of two logs, wrapped my bloody, broken wrists, and took me to the hospital in the small town nearby. From there, an ambulance took me to another hospital in the capital, an hour away. My mom went back to the farm to take care of the unfinished chores.

When I finally woke up from the surgery, it was early evening. I didn't see my mom until later that night—it took her hours to finish all the chores. But when she came, she brought me dinner. For the next two months, she came twice a day, every single day, bringing me lunch and dinner because she knew I hated the hospital food.

This, I believe, is love. This is my mom's way of expressing her feelings.

I never thought about this until I came to America and discovered a different way of living. I liked it, and I changed. I now say hi to strangers on the street, smile at people I don't know, and I tell my husband I love him without feeling embarrassed.

I wanted my mom to change, too, so I wrote her a letter, where, for the first time, I opened up to her. And for the first time, I told her I loved her. My mom never responded.

That was several years ago. I have learned many things since then. I have learned that words don't always hold true and that actions are often stronger than words. I have learned to accept that my mom will never change: she will never tell me she loves me. But I have also learned that that is okay, for she has proven it many times—by showing, not telling.

Showing love, I believe, is stronger than a million uttered words could ever be.

ANN ERIK was born in Estonia and came to the United States at the age of nineteen to work as a nanny for a year. Eleven years later, she's still in the United States, married, living in New Jersey, and working as a personal trainer and a group fitness coordinator at a local health club. Her mother calls her every Sunday.

A Tender Lullaby

LEE REEVES

I believe in singing badly.

When I was eight years old I stood in line with my peers waiting to audition for the school's Christmas choir. Each of us was required to sing "Three Blind Mice" for Sister Anthony, who had the thankless job of triaging over fifty third-graders according to their apparent musical talents.

I remember how nervous I felt as I moved toward the front of the line, barely able to breathe when it was my turn. Sister Anthony blew a note from the small, circular pitch pipe she carried in her pocket and nudged me to hurry up. I squeaked out the first two lines, "Three blind mice, three blind mice," and she raised the palm of her hand to my face.

"That's enough, Marylee," she said, and pointed to the back of the room where I joined a cadre of losers who spent the remainder of the audition making trouble.

This was by no means the most traumatic event of my life, but it did silence me for many years, convincing me that I was not a natural singer, therefore not meant to sing.

That same year in religion class, I got an opposing message when a nun told us the story about a monk who crooned to God with the abandon of a small child, despite his terrible voice. The other monks whose voices soared with angelic perfection shunned him. They raised their eyebrows and glared, but he was oblivious to their disgust. He wasn't singing for them but for God, who was immensely pleased. The human flaws of the monk's voice could not be heard in heaven, only the pure pitch of his love and intention.

My courage to sing returned when my first child was born. She was sick much of the time with raging fevers and infections resulting from a rare blood disorder. For hours every afternoon when she was a baby, I held Leta while we danced to the tender cadence of Rod Stewart's love song, "You're In My Heart." I'd sing to her in the softest voice I could muster, off-key and imperfectly. She'd gaze at me like I was a goddess. Often when it seemed she'd fallen asleep, I'd stop singing. Then she would open her eyes and gently tap her tiny hand on my breast. I'd pick up the song at a favorite line, and she would lay her head down again.

Leta grew into a beautiful young woman. But at age twenty, she developed leukemia. Now she's gone, and I spend much of my time writing the story of her brief time on earth. I remind myself that my voice and writing—just as in singing—need not be perfect. As I pour it onto the page I must accept its limitations and flaws. Far more important is the love and intention I bring to the process.

Sometimes, I imagine that Leta can still hear me, that my voice wafts across the veil and touches her like a tender lullaby.

LEE REEVES is part-time director of the National Neutropenia Network, a charitable organization for individuals and families affected by neutropenia, the rare disease her daughter was born with. Ms. Reeves is also working on a book about her daughter's life.

The Yellow House

JULIE M. SELLERS

I followed my memories down the rutted road one rainy, late summer day. As I parked in front of the little yellow lake house and slid from my seat, I pictured the house as it had been the last time I'd seen it, over a decade before.

I loved that house as much as I loved him, I think. When he gave me my own key, you would have thought it was the key to his heart, I was so happy. I sanded, painted, wall-papered, and picked out furniture from thrift stores. Soon the house—the interior, at least—began to take shape.

Outside, the house was still a bit rough around the edges. I envisioned restoring it to its original sunny yellow when the spring came. But the spring didn't come, at least for the two of us. We parted ways just as the buds were forming on the trees.

He made his life with another, and for ten years I avoided this place. I didn't want to see my little yellow house, home to someone else, with some other woman's curtains hanging in the kitchen window I painted shut and had to pry open from the outside.

So I leaned against my wet bumper that day in hope that I could move on, at last. I'd expected to find that the house, at least, had moved on without me. But what I saw was not a cheery light in the window or flower boxes along the porch.

I found boarded-up windows and rotten boards. The house looked as forlorn and forgotten as I. It looked as if it should be knocked down, or as if soon a strong breeze would take care of doing just that and save a bulldozer the trouble. But as I stared through the bleak light I remembered my haven as it had been—remembered myself as I had been—and I realized something.

The house would never have been a palace, but it at least deserved a chance. Now my heart broke for what it had become. It could still have been what it always was; the only thing missing these last years was the care.

I believe we have to take care of things: our homes, our families, our loves—and most important, one another.

Because if we don't do it every day, week after week, year after year, no matter how much we were once loved, we eventually fall to ruin.

Kudos are not given to those among us who take care of the day to day, the mundane, the runny noses, and rotten fence posts. There are no awards for those who love well or amply provide for those who need them. There is no acclaim for those of us who just stay.

My trip to rid myself of the little yellow house didn't go as planned, but I did learn. While she is down, she's not out. Seldom are things broken beyond repair, even though it may seem at first as though they are. With effort, she could be a haven once again, just maybe not for me. She's holding on, still waiting for the spring to come, and so, I guess, am I.

JULIE M. SELLERS is a human resources manager and, more important, mother of two wonderful children, Sophie and Max. Her first book, *Immediate Family: The Adoption Option*, chronicles her experiences as a single parent who adopted two children from Russia. Ms. Sellers lives in Indiana with her daughter, her son, two dogs, one guinea pig, and a turtle.

A Powerful Act of Love

∽

SUSAN HALL

It showed up last Christmas, a gift borne by eager grandparents. Long and unwieldy, we managed it through the front door, grandparents on the porch, I inside, angling it this way and that.

Since the unwrapped present's box boldly declared its contents, I dispensed with the usual wait-until-Christmas rule. We pried apart the box's sharp staples, and there it was: the mother of all electronic keyboards.

My son loves music. Diagnosed at age one with a rare seizure disorder that stalled his cognitive development, he is fond of rhythm, buttons, and lights. And so we have known some keyboards over the years. They've been presents from all over the place: eBay, garage sales, a local grocery store. Our basement is a bone yard of broken keyboards, some still working erratically if pounded in the right spots.

The new present was spectacular. A song bank stores one hundred familiar tunes. By pressing a sequence of buttons, my son can change the instruments and tones in startling ways. We've heard everything from "Ode to Joy" with a disco beat to a haunting church organ rendition of "Happy Birthday."

I love the keyboard not because my son loves it, not because it is a great educational toy, but because it safely occupies him for long stretches. As long as I hear the stops and starts of the music blaring from my son's room, I have time to fold towels, grade a paper, throw a roast in the oven, or read about my son's disability. I have time to fantasize about mounting some public and terrific response to my son's affliction. The keyboards have been great babysitters.

One day I wandered into my son's room. "Beautiful Dreamer" was playing. I sat down on the floor to cut my toenails. My son leaned back and flashed me a beatific smile. I smiled back: the music was nice, the piano just right.

A few days later my son, insistent, led me to the bathroom connected to his bedroom. He climbed up on the toilet and reached into a basket perched on the windowsill. Then he handed me a pair of nail clippers. Instantly I understood.

And so I sat for a while on his bedroom floor, just listening with him. "Four-four," I requested, naming the number for my favorite tune, "Red River Valley."

He surprised me by accommodating my request, and we shared some smiles. As we listened, the sunlight came streaming through the blinds. It was brilliant and perfect and infused with that certain and unnamable something else.

The other day, curious, I looked up the lyrics to "Red River Valley."

> Come and sit by my side if you love me,
> Do not hasten to bid me adieu.

And so I have come to believe in sitting and listening with someone as a powerful act, a loving action full with possibility. This I have learned from my son and his special music, a belief forged only after I was able to take a moment and listen.

SUSAN HALL is a high school English teacher. She lives with her husband and two children in Pentwater, Michigan, where she and her family enjoy cheering on her son's Special Olympics basketball team, the Area 24 Tornadoes.

Pennies from Heaven

REG STARK

I lost count at three hundred. There have been shiny ones, tarnished ones, mangled ones, and vintage ones: pennies from heaven.

Linda, my wife of forty-three years, lost her courageous battle with cancer over a year ago, and ever since then I have been finding a penny almost every day.

The first one was in the parking lot of the local post office, about a month after Linda's passing. I was there to mail a stack of bills—a new experience for me. Linda had always handled our money, and as a member of the accounting department for an insurance company, she was good at it. I, on the other hand, was not to be trusted with such matters.

Whenever Linda found a penny, she would put it in her shoe for luck. If I saw one, I didn't think it was worth the trouble to bend down to pick it up. But that day I took the penny home and put it in a jar in the kitchen. It was not until I had to get a bigger jar that I began to realize that something was going on.

I found one six different times at Bush International Airport in Houston, the city where I live. Each penny was in the same place underneath the same chair where I put my shoes back on after going through security. In fact, I find one in every airport I travel through.

There is a story for every found penny. Many times all I have to do is ask and one will appear. I have been stopped in my tracks by something or someone steering me in a different way only to find a penny waiting for me.

And it's not just me. Our son, Jeff; my sister-in-law, Mary; and my best friend, Tom, have all told me of finding pennies at times when they needed a boost.

Linda was known for her generosity, acute pragmatism, and tuna salad. She was a caring, doting mother to our wonderful son and a loving, devoted wife to me. She enjoyed a good, raunchy joke; had a bawdy laugh; and could demonstrate a sailor's vocabulary whenever her Irish was tested.

We all watched as she deteriorated over a long, agonizing six months in and out of surgery and chemotherapy—without a complaint or a hint of self-pity. She finally succumbed one evening just before midnight in a home she loved—surrounded by her friends and family.

I have always had a long-distance relationship with God—doubting more than believing. But now I believe those pennies keep bolstering an unshakable faith—although I backed into it. Someone told me angels leave pennies to remind you they are with you. I think that first penny was a pat on the back for getting those bills out on time—for a job well done. All the rest have proven to me that Linda is still with me.

Yes, you could say that I am now penny-wise.

REG STARK was born in Beaumont, Texas. Since retiring from his career as a project developer in the health-care field, he has pursued his lifelong dream as a full-time artist. Mr. Stark and his wife, Linda, were high school sweethearts and were married for forty-three years. They have one son, Jeff, a successful graphic artist and designer who lives with Mr. Stark in Sugar Land, Texas.

Who We Really Are Inside

∽

MATTHEW SCHMIDT

"I'm gay," she cried. "I'm gay."

It was early, around two or three a.m. shortly after Thanksgiving, when my mother told me over the phone. I gagged; it was like a reflex after a near-death collision. Years of pent-up aggression and adrenaline crashed out of my system. I wanted to vomit. And to have her hold me.

At the time I was deep in a manic-depressive cycle (though I did not know it then), and I was suicidal. As I lay curled into the fetal position on my bed, in a full panic attack, my wife forced me to call my mother. Why my mother? Because despite everything she had put us through, she was still the only person I could remotely consider sharing my own shame and fear with.

For a long time I carried inside myself a terrible weight of anger at my mother's apparent abandonment of my family and me when she suddenly moved out of the house when I was twenty-five. I tried to prod my mom to tell me what was wrong. But all I got in return was a fist-clenching tantrum and blood-curdling moan begging us to stop pushing her to tell us if she was coming home and to stop pushing her to talk about what was going on inside. Even worse than these moments was the silence that followed: the weeks without contact, knowing only that mom was suffering and that I didn't know how to help. And that she would not, could not, tell me why.

Then early that November morning, after calling her to demand answers because I was scared and suicidal, and because I needed her, she told me. She moaned the words, like she was giving birth to them: "I'm gay."

I burst into tears, gulping air into my lungs. But from somewhere just as deep came a sense of relief with each shudder of my body. "Finally," I thought, "an explanation!" And that meant a means to reconnect with her. She was different now, but somehow more herself than ever.

This experience changed us all—my parents, my siblings, and me. It shattered the masks behind which we had hidden our deepest selves from one another. And when we saw one another—raw and vulnerable—we reacted by offering support and forgiveness. We didn't run away in fear that seeing the truth might expose our own frailties to one another. We let go of our illusions: my mother and father about their marriage and me about my own, which later ended in divorce. We saw in the letting go that there was a new love waiting beyond the illusion.

So I believe in the power of people to forgive and the survival of the love between them through even the most wrenching assaults of anger and mistrust. Although the classically "nuclear" family in which I was raised would never again exist as it had, I believe it will survive the divorce of my parents. My father—the man with whom my mother bore me, three other sons, and a daughter, and whose hand she held as two of those sons were buried—has come to forgive her and understand her. And love her.

So whatever else is to come, I believe that this forgiveness of one another will bind us together as a new family, in a new form with new members. The essence at the heart of that love will be there: acceptance.

MATTHEW SCHMIDT learned most of the important lessons of life growing up on his family's dairy farm in Kansas. Anything else he knows he learned studying in Los Angeles, Washington, D.C., and Eastern Europe. Mr. Schmidt is an assistant professor at the School of Advanced Military Studies at Fort Leavenworth.

Creation Is the Creator

VICKI WATSON

I grew up on a small family farm in the Texas blackland prairie where mockingbirds sang and bluebonnets bloomed. The land was kind, the neighbors friendly, and my parents loving.

The main lesson my parents taught their children was to "take care of the land and your neighbors, and they'll take care of you." My mother loved to say:

> There is a destiny that makes us brothers,
> None goes his way alone;
> What we send into the lives of others,
> Comes back into our own.

When neighbors were sick or hurt, my parents and others tended their land, took them food, and cared for their children. They worked with scouts and 4-H, had the local baseball field in their yard, and tutored neighbor kids along with their own, helping them make bug and leaf collections for school. They worked the polls at election time and helped maintain our small, rural school. They took care of their community.

And they took care of their land. Although our farm was pretty flat, my father dutifully contour-plowed around every little bump. He and my mother hand-weeded thorny mesquite to keep it from spreading. They fought the dumping of raw sewage in the creek that ran through our land. They were proud of their native prairie pastures, their gentle, well-cared-for livestock, and our farm's abundant wildlife. In the 1950s, a small flock of whooping cranes landed on our farm pond. Years later, I learned that this flock represented most of the remaining cranes at that time. We didn't know what they were, and my dad considered shooting one to take in for identification. But he couldn't do it. "They were too 'purty' to shoot," he said.

My parents did not inherit their land but bought it with help from the U.S. Federal Land Bank. They paid their taxes willingly, seeing the benefits of public schools, roads, police and fire protection, and programs that helped the poor and elderly and helped people like them get their start.

Our family's entertainment consisted of weenie roasts on the creek, watching sunsets, listening to bobwhites calling, making Texas mustang grape jelly, and picking dewberries for cobbler and homemade ice cream. We sang "America the Beautiful" because we knew that America, the land and the community, took care of us.

When I went off to college, my childhood love of the land and its people grew into the professions of ecology, teaching, and community service. The lessons I learned on that blackland prairie farm have served me throughout life.

I was taught to revere and delight in all of creation; that there is divinity in all things. I believe that creation is the Creator, continually re-creating itself. We humans are a part of that, shaping our environment and communities. Humans have become one of the most powerful forces on earth. And as we wield that power, we must always remember, "What we send into the lives of others, comes back into our own."

Born in 1953 on a small family farm, VICKI WATSON grew up watching her parents' loving care for land and community. After earning a PhD in ecology, Ms. Watson became a University of Montana environmental studies professor, focusing on watershed conservation and helping citizens work for the sustainable, ethical use of water.

The Power of Friendship

NADIA ANN HENDERSON

When I was in the sixth grade, my class was assigned to be buddies with first- and second-grade kids. I got this little Spanish girl named Shelsey. She was the cutest little girl that I had ever seen, with chubby cheeks and big brown eyes. She was small for her age, and she didn't play with most kids that were in her class. She basically isolated herself from the rest of the world. Shelsey's eyes were lifeless, and her demeanor was cold and unfeeling.

I tried all sorts of things to get her to talk to me— including bribery. I brought her toys and Barbie dolls and crayons and all sorts of things. But try as I might, nothing worked. One time, I gave her a coloring book and said, "Look Shelsey, now you can color all the time and you won't have to worry about wasting paper anymore."

She looked down at the coloring book and then looked at me, and then finally looked away. By that time I was just truly and utterly frustrated. I didn't know how I was going to get through to her, but I was determined to try.

It continued for a couple of more months, this whole "you don't exist" phase. She wouldn't look at me or talk to me. She would just stare off into space. So one Friday, I decided to tell her a story about my childhood and what it was like. If I was going to get through to her, then now was my moment when no one was around and we were just one-on-one. It was me to her.

I told her that I felt isolated from my fellow classmates, and how I thought only my teachers liked me simply because I was the only one in my class who didn't have a mother. I confided to Shelsey that I felt every day was a battle as I fought back tears so people wouldn't know how much I was hurting.

She sat there just listening, trying to decide whether I was lying or not. Finally, when my story ended, there were tears in her eyes and she was shaking. And then she did the unthinkable. She said, "Thank you." From then on, she was a different little girl. She started smiling and laughing and interacting with the other kids.

Looking back at this I'm in awe, because all it took for me to get her out of her shell was to help her realize that she wasn't alone and didn't have to pretend to be alone.

I didn't ask her to tell her story, because her story is my story. Her childhood was exactly like mine. And she finally realized that I understood her and I knew what she was going through and that it was okay to let the burden that she had on her little shoulders go.

You ask me what I believe in? I believe in the power of love and friendship and how it can cure even the worst of heartaches and pain.

NADIA ANN HENDERSON is a sophomore at Washington State University in Pullman, where she is pursuing a degree in veterinary medicine. Ms. Henderson devotes much of her time to being a college student and to helping abused animals find new homes.

To Love the Person in Front of Me

KARLA GERGEN

Although I love my job, it is not an easy one. I teach eighth grade at a small middle school for kids who need more than our large, urban school systems can provide. Their histories and needs are challenging, and this can often lead to difficult behavior of one kind or another.

One young girl will always stand out in my mind. At one point, she told me about horrific abuse she was experiencing at home. I was able to help change the situation, but this type of abuse causes far-reaching and permanent damage. Although I knew she could be innocent and kind, this young woman antagonized me when she was in my classroom.

She often laughed at her classmates and at me. She rolled her eyes when I gave her directions, and then only sometimes chose to follow them. When I told the class that another teacher would be leaving the school, she looked at me and said, "I wish you were leaving instead."

I was a young teacher working an exhausting job, and I often lost my patience, especially with her. My only lasting frustration was that I didn't remember why she acted the way she did and respond with more love. I sometimes wondered how she remembered me.

In the back of my room, I posted a favorite saying by Mother Teresa: "We can do no great things, only small things with great love." There were many days when, feeling discouraged, my eyes would fall upon that quote. "Love," I reminded, and commanded, myself. I believe that loving those who are the most difficult to love is the hardest and most important work of my life. Usually, at the end of the day, all I can say is that I've tried. I pray that my students know I did my best and that they forgive me for all the times I didn't.

One day at lunch not too long ago, some other teachers and I were talking about a local young man who had become a well-known professional athlete. I took pride in claiming him as a former student from a previous job. And then the thought occurred to me that most of my current students were unlikely to achieve that same level of status. I was ashamed to find that fact bothered me, but it did.

That same afternoon, the young woman I mentioned earlier happened to visit our school with a friend of hers. When she saw me, she immediately smiled and said, "This is the teacher I was telling you about, the one who helped me."

I almost started crying at my own stupidity. I realized I would not trade all the professional sports players in the world for this one young woman and her memory of me.

At the end of the day, at the end of our lives, the worldly definition of greatness is an illusion. All I need to do is love the person in front of me. Maybe they'll come back some day and tell me it mattered. Most likely they won't.

My life won't appear in history books, but it will remain in the hearts of those I have loved. I could not ask for a better legacy.

KARLA GERGEN loves her job as a middle school teacher despite the shock and disbelief of most people when she tells them this. After teaching for a decade in Minnesota, she moved to Honduras and is currently teaching eighth grade language arts and social studies at a bilingual school in San Pedro Sula.

Love from Head to Toe

LORENA TEMPLETON QUERNS

I believe that love is a choice. I have seen that choice made in my own home, and I know the difference it makes.

When I was fourteen and my sisters were eleven and nine, we adopted my little brother, Tyler James. My parents had wanted another baby for a long time. When a baby didn't come through pregnancy or adoption, my mom started praying for God to take the desire for a baby away.

Finally, she felt like He did. She had just started a new job when we received a call from the daughter of a family friend. She told us that she loved her baby very much but could not take care of him in the way that he deserved.

She knew my parents had wanted a baby for a long time, and she had seen the way they loved my sisters and me.

A family meeting was called, and my parents consulted us on the new prospect. The decision was made to adopt this tiny baby, because as my parents said, "If God drops a baby in your lap, what can you do? Say no, I don't want it?"

Although the decision to adopt Tyler may have been a natural one, loving him did not come as naturally at first for my mother. She was confused because she had finally become satisfied with her life without another baby. There were times when my mom held him and felt guilty because she did not feel the same intensity of love for him as she had for us.

Even though she didn't feel the same love for Tyler at first, she chose to love him anyway. She did this by taking care of him, singing to him, holding him, and talking to him. She loved him by changing his dirty diapers and getting out of bed at four in the morning when he cried. She behaved the same way she did with me when I was a baby, although she may not have felt the same way. Soon, the feelings of love joined the behavior of love.

Today, Tyler is nearly eleven and has been officially ours for nine years now. The only thing that makes him any different from his sisters is that he celebrates Gotcha Day, the day of his adoption, every April. Our mom and dad love all of us the same.

Often my mom can be heard telling Tyler, "I love you from the top of your head, to the tips of your toes, and everything in between," and she means it as much as she did when she said it to me as a child. More important, Tyler's response of "even up to the sky" shows he knows it as much as I did. Many of my friends are shocked when they find out that my little brother is adopted, because he looks like he belongs in our family. And of course, that's because he does, because we chose to love.

LORENA TEMPLETON QUERNS teaches middle school language arts at a Christian school in New Jersey. She and her husband, Steve, live in Pennsylvania, where she enjoys reading, crocheting, and painting. Her brother, Tyler, lives next door and loves to spend time with his big sister and brother-in-law.

Made by Hand

MARY MRUGALSKI

I believe in baking hearty, healthy, whole wheat bread, preferably with someone I love, for someone I love.

The first time I made whole wheat bread, I was twenty years old, pregnant, and unmarried. My boyfriend and I were experimenting back then, trying different things. Baking bread was part of the process. After growing up on bologna and white bread, we wanted more, more substance to our bread and our lives. We were changing the world and relationships. Who needed marriage? Make love, not war. When the father of my child said we were soul mates, I believed him. I even thought that I knew the exact moment we conceived.

Then I told him that I was gaining weight for a reason, and he panicked. He pleaded with me to "take care of our problem." I was confused. I thought we were soul mates. I thought that this was meant to be. But it was a problem for him. He disappeared, and I made bread.

Making bread healed my pain. It felt healthy and honest and pure; whole wheat, not white. It had substance and character. The dough felt sticky at first, like "our problem." But the more I worked with it, the better it felt. And the better I felt about what had become "my problem."

Of course "my problem" was no problem at all. My child was a gift. His flyaway dandelion hair never quite knew which direction to grow in. He taught me to roller skate. I taught him to ride a bike. He taught me to play pinball.

And I taught him to make bread. I made the big loaf. He made the little one. "Hey, let's swirl it with cinnamon and sugar, or cheese," he'd say. And we did. That bread bound us together and filled the emptiness that snuck in when no one was looking.

Bread baking became a tradition with both my children. We would always bake bread when it rained outside or felt like a storm inside our family.

We've been busy lately helping my daughter heal from a long illness. Life has been about driving to doctors and classes and working and cleaning and laundry and errands and struggling and searching for balance. One day when

I panicked about trying to get everything done in a weekend, the bread of my past returned.

Then I opened up the jar of whole wheat flour and once again began to heal. As I kneaded and pushed and shaped that dough, I began to unwind. I prayed silently to heal the person who would receive this bread. The sticky dough became tender inside my hands.

Time began to expand, and the day felt luxuriously long. No more panicking. The baking bread smelled like comfort and safety. I made the big loaf; my daughter made the small one.

I believe in the power of healing, hearty, whole wheat bread, made by hand with love.

MARY MRUGALSKI delivered news on Chicago radio for more than a decade under the name Mary Anne Meyers. She now produces news stories from home, allowing her to bake even more bread for family and friends. Her two grown children occasionally take time from their busy lives to visit and knead a loaf or two.

A Dog's Life

FRED FLAXMAN

I believe I learned everything I needed to know about how to live the good life from my childhood dog, Buster.

If you want your young child to learn responsibility, get him a dog. That's what conventional wisdom teaches. And it was true in my case. But Buster also taught me more about irresponsibility than any human I've ever met.

When I was eight, I convinced my mother, who hates animals, to buy me a beagle. We got 50 percent off on Buster because he had stiff hind legs and undescended testicles. It taught my mom to be wary of bargains.

Buster lasted for fourteen years and died of old age with a little assistance from the veterinarian and the approval of my mother. During his last few, flatulent years, my mother took care of him completely since, by that time, I was away at college.

But for ten years I walked Buster twice a day—in rain, snow, or shine, like an old-fashioned mailman. I fed him, brushed him, petted him, and took care of him. I also confided in him, and he became my best friend.

I learned to be a responsible adult, just as conventional wisdom predicted. I married and had two children. For more than four decades, I went to work each day, putting up gracefully with rush hours, boring meetings, budgets, and personnel problems caused, presumably, by employees who had been deprived of dogs when they were children.

I footed the bills for my family's food, clothing, shelter, and college education. I even paid for their mistakes. I washed and dried the dishes and occasionally made the beds. I even contributed to charities. I don't think I could have been much more responsible.

But, all along, I harbored a secret desire to lead the good life Buster introduced me to. He never put in a full day's work. He never even worked part-time. He never earned a dime, never did anything useful, never married or had children or knew or cared if he did, never put up with traffic, never sat through a meeting, never prepared a budget, never read a book or a newspaper, never washed a car, never wasted time watching television, and never worried about nuclear war—or anything else for that matter except, perhaps, which tree he should choose for his next stop. And even that he did without first obtaining an environmental impact report.

Buster was beautifully, innocently, and completely irresponsible. And I loved him as he was, for what he was.

My former colleagues at work would be surprised to learn that all I ever really wanted out of life was to have my back scratched while sitting in front of the TV, like Buster, to run free in the woods on a sunny summer day, and to curl up in front of a fire on a cold winter's evening, listening to classical music that someone else would put on the stereo.

Having a dog for fourteen years may have taught me how to be responsible. But Buster taught me how to live.

FRED FLAXMAN is the author of *Sixty Slices of Life . . . on Wry: The Private Life of a Public Broadcaster,* from which this essay was adapted. He is also the producer and host of *Compact Discoveries,* an internationally distributed public radio music series. He has never owned another dog.

How to Write Your Own
This I Believe Essay

We invite you to contribute to this project by writing and submitting your own statement of personal belief. We understand how challenging this is—it requires such intimacy that you may find it difficult to begin. To guide you through this process, we offer these suggestions:

Tell a story. Be specific. Take your belief out of the ether and ground it in the events of your life. Your story need not be heart-warming or gut-wrenching—it can even be funny—but it should be real. Consider moments when your belief was formed, tested, or changed. Make sure your story ties to the essence of your daily life philosophy and to the shaping of your beliefs.

Be brief. Your statement should be between 350 and 500 words. The shorter length forces you to focus on the belief that is central to your life.

Name your belief. If you can't name it in a sentence or two, your essay might not be about belief. Rather than writing a list, consider focusing on one core belief.

Be positive. Say what you *do* believe, not what you *don't* believe. Avoid statements of religious dogma, preaching, or editorializing.

Be personal. Make your essay about you; speak in the first person. Try reading your essay aloud to yourself several times, and each time edit it and simplify it until you find the words, tone, and story that truly echo your belief and the way you speak.

Please submit your completed essay to the *This I Believe* project by visiting the Web site, www.thisibelieve.org. We are eager for your contribution.

ACKNOWLEDGMENTS

First, we offer our deepest thanks to the essayists who contributed their personal statements to this book. We honor their willingness to explore and express the things that matter most.

In reviving *This I Believe* we owe a debt of gratitude to Casey Murrow, Keith Wheelock, and Margot Wheelock Schlegel, the children of *This I Believe* creators Edward R. Murrow and Ward Wheelock. Our project continues to be guided by Edward R. Murrow and his team, which preceded us in the 1950s: Gladys Chang Hardy, Reny Hill, Donald J. Merwin, Edward P. Morgan, Raymond Swing, and Ward Wheelock.

Our special thanks to Atlantic Public Media, Inc., in Woods Hole, Massachusetts, where many of these essays were originally reviewed.

For their advice and assistance, we acknowledge our This I Believe, Inc., board of directors: David Langstaff, John Y. Brown III, Marty Bollinger, Jerry Howe, Lynn Amato Madonna, and Declan Murphy.

Our current on-air home is *The Bob Edwards Show* on Sirius XM Satellite Radio/*Bob Edwards Weekend* on Public Radio International. Enormous thanks go to Bob Edwards and his fine staff: Steve Lickteig, Geoffrey Redick, Ed McNulty, Ariana Pekary, Shelley Tillman, Dan Bloom, Andy Danyo, Chad Campbell, and Cristy Meiners. At Sirius XM, we thank Jeremy Coleman, Frank Raphael, and Kevin Straley.

We also want to express our thanks to everyone at NPR, which aired our radio series for four years, especially Jay Kernis, Stacey Foxwell, and Robert Spier, our steadfast supporters through thick and thin.

Without our funders, our project simply would not be possible. *This I Believe* received the first faithful leap of funding from the Corporation for Public Broadcasting. Over the years, we have also received corporate underwriting from Farmers Insurance, Capella University, Prudential Retirement, E.ON U.S., and, most recently, Kellogg's Corn Flakes. In addition, we have received grants from the Righteous Persons Foundation and the Prudential Foundation. We are also extremely grateful for donations from individuals who support our programming and mission.

The comprehensive Web site for *This I Believe* (thisibelieve .org) was built by Dennis Whiteman at Fastpipe Media, Inc., and was designed by the folks at LeapFrog Interactive with help from Chris Enander of TBD Design. Our iPhone app was cocreated by Dennis along with Wayne Walrath at Acme Technologies.

The creation of this book was immeasurably aided by our agent, Andrew Blauner, of Blauner Books Literary Agency. We are fortunate to have had his able services and his unwavering support.

Our publisher, John Wiley & Sons, has been tremendously supportive of our recent publishing activities. Our hats are off to editor Hana Lane and her whole team for making this process as painless, indeed as pleasurable, as possible.

And, finally, we thank the thousands of individuals who have accepted our invitation to write and share their own personal statements of belief. This book contains but a fraction of the many thoughtful and inspiring essays that have been submitted to our project, and we are grateful for them all. We invite you to join this group by writing your own *This I Believe* essay and submitting it to us via our Web site, thisibelieve.org. You will find instructions in the appendix of this book on how to do so.